OPPOSING
VIEWPOINTS®

# DISCRIMINATION

# Other Books of Related Interest

OPPOSING
VIEWPOINTS®

# DISCRIMINATION

Mary E. Williams, *Book Editor*

Daniel Leone, *President*
Bonnie Szumski, *Publisher*
Scott Barbour, *Managing Editor*

OPPOSING
VIEWPOINTS®
SERIES

GREENHAVEN
PRESS®

THOMSON
™
GALE

San Diego • Detroit • New York • San Francisco • Cleveland
New Haven, Conn. • Waterville, Maine • London • Munich

© 2003 by Greenhaven Press. Greenhaven Press is an imprint of The Gale Group, Inc., a division of Thomson Learning, Inc.

Greenhaven® and Thomson Learning™ are trademarks used herein under license.

*For more information, contact*
Greenhaven Press
27500 Drake Rd.
Farmington Hills, MI 48331-3535
Or you can visit our Internet site at http://www.gale.com

Cover credit: © Photodisk

**LIBRARY OF CONGRESS CATALOGING-IN-PUBLICATION DATA**

Discrimination / Mary E. Williams, book editor.
    p. cm. — (Opposing viewpoints series)
 Includes bibliographical references and index.
 ISBN 0-7377-1225-2 (pbk. : alk. paper) —
 ISBN 0-7377-1226-0 (lib. bdg. : alk. paper)
    1. Discrimination—United States. 2. Minorities—United States. 3. Reverse discrimination—United States. [1. Discrimination. 2. Reverse discrimination. 3. Affirmative action programs.] I. Williams, Mary E., 1960– II. Opposing viewpoints series (Unnumbered)
 JC599.U5 D56  2003
 305—dc21                                        2001008677

Printed in the United States of America

"Congress shall make
no law. . . abridging the
freedom of speech, or of
the press."

*First Amendment to the U.S. Constitution*

The basic foundation of our democracy is the First
Amendment guarantee of freedom of expression.
The Opposing Viewpoints Series is dedicated to the
concept of this basic freedom and the idea that it is
more important to practice it than to enshrine it.

# Contents

# Why Consider Opposing Viewpoints?

*"The only way in which a human being can make some approach to knowing the whole of a subject is by hearing what can be said about it by persons of every variety of opinion and studying all modes in which it can be looked at by every character of mind. No wise man ever acquired his wisdom in any mode but this."*

John Stuart Mill

In our media-intensive culture it is not difficult to find differing opinions. Thousands of newspapers and magazines and dozens of radio and television talk shows resound with differing points of view. The difficulty lies in deciding which opinion to agree with and which "experts" seem the most credible. The more inundated we become with differing opinions and claims, the more essential it is to hone critical reading and thinking skills to evaluate these ideas. Opposing Viewpoints books address this problem directly by presenting stimulating debates that can be used to enhance and teach these skills. The varied opinions contained in each book examine many different aspects of a single issue. While examining these conveniently edited opposing views, readers can develop critical thinking skills such as the ability to compare and contrast authors' credibility, facts, argumentation styles, use of persuasive techniques, and other stylistic tools. In short, the Opposing Viewpoints Series is an ideal way to attain the higher-level thinking and reading skills so essential in a culture of diverse and contradictory opinions.

In addition to providing a tool for critical thinking, Opposing Viewpoints books challenge readers to question their own strongly held opinions and assumptions. Most people form their opinions on the basis of upbringing, peer pressure, and personal, cultural, or professional bias. By reading carefully balanced opposing views, readers must directly confront new ideas as well as the opinions of those with whom they disagree. This is not to simplistically argue that everyone who reads opposing views will—or should—change his or her opinion. Instead, the series enhances readers' understanding of their own views by encouraging confrontation with opposing ideas. Careful examination of others' views can lead to the readers' understanding of the logical inconsistencies in their own opinions, perspective on why they hold an opinion, and the consideration of the possibility that their opinion requires further evaluation.

## Evaluating Other Opinions

To ensure that this type of examination occurs, Opposing Viewpoints books present all types of opinions. Prominent spokespeople on different sides of each issue as well as well-known professionals from many disciplines challenge the reader. An additional goal of the series is to provide a forum for other, less known, or even unpopular viewpoints. The opinion of an ordinary person who has had to make the decision to cut off life support from a terminally ill relative, for example, may be just as valuable and provide just as much insight as a medical ethicist's professional opinion. The editors have two additional purposes in including these less known views. One, the editors encourage readers to respect others' opinions—even when not enhanced by professional credibility. It is only by reading or listening to and objectively evaluating others' ideas that one can determine whether they are worthy of consideration. Two, the inclusion of such viewpoints encourages the important critical thinking skill of objectively evaluating an author's credentials and bias. This evaluation will illuminate an author's reasons for taking a particular stance on an issue and will aid in readers' evaluation of the author's ideas.

It is our hope that these books will give readers a deeper understanding of the issues debated and an appreciation of the complexity of even seemingly simple issues when good and honest people disagree. This awareness is particularly important in a democratic society such as ours in which people enter into public debate to determine the common good. Those with whom one disagrees should not be regarded as enemies but rather as people whose views deserve careful examination and may shed light on one's own.

Thomas Jefferson once said that "difference of opinion leads to inquiry, and inquiry to truth." Jefferson, a broadly educated man, argued that "if a nation expects to be ignorant and free . . . it expects what never was and never will be." As individuals and as a nation, it is imperative that we consider the opinions of others and examine them with skill and discernment. The Opposing Viewpoints Series is intended to help readers achieve this goal.

David L. Bender and Bruno Leone,
Founders

———————————

Greenhaven Press anthologies primarily consist of previously published material taken from a variety of sources, including periodicals, books, scholarly journals, newspapers, government documents, and position papers from private and public organizations. These original sources are often edited for length and to ensure their accessibility for a young adult audience. The anthology editors also change the original titles of these works in order to clearly present the main thesis of each viewpoint and to explicitly indicate the opinion presented in the viewpoint. These alterations are made in consideration of both the reading and comprehension levels of a young adult audience. Every effort is made to ensure that Greenhaven Press accurately reflects the original intent of the authors included in this anthology.

———————————

# Introduction

*"Fundamental fairness demands that steps be taken to prohibit [racial] profiling in theory and in practice."*

—*John Lamberth*

*"Racial profiling . . . is a tool, and often an effective one, in police work."*

—*Woody West*

"It was the state trooper's eyes that worried me most," writes *Washington Post* reporter Darryl Fears as he recounts his disturbing experience of being pulled over while driving on the Kansas Turnpike. "They were wide and filled with fear. He advanced on my car with an awkward gait, like a man walking on a ledge: one hand on the black handle of his holstered gun, the other held out beside him, flat and steady. He was balancing himself, I thought with a sudden chill, so he'd be ready if he needed to draw his weapon and shoot."

Fears, a black man with dreadlocks, had ostensibly been pulled over for speeding and for neglecting to signal as he changed lanes. While showing his license and registration, Fears attempted to make the trooper more comfortable by engaging in polite conversation—talking about how he had just left a job at the *Los Angeles Times* and was driving across country to a new job in Washington, D.C. When the trooper asked him for his current address, Fears pulled out a welcome letter from his new workplace and a note from an agency that was to provide him temporary accommodations until he found a permanent home. The trooper seemed to grow more suspicious, asking him, "[Is there] any reason why you're moving to so many places in so little time?" and "You wouldn't happen to have a gun or any drugs in there, would you?" When Fears explained that he had no weapons or drugs, the trooper, along with a sheriff's deputy who had pulled up to join the interrogation, asked to search the inside of his car. Fears refused, countering that the officers needed a warrant to do that. The deputy then brought out a police dog to sniff the outside of the vehicle, telling Fears that "if there was even a seed to be found . . . the dog would 'scratch up'" his car. In the end, the dog detected nothing and Fears was given a written warning for speeding and failing to signal properly.

Fears's experience is not uncommon. Many African American and Latino motorists claim that they have been stopped and searched by law enforcement officers without probable cause. Furthermore, observers point out, racial minorities are stopped by police far more often than white people are—especially if they are driving pricey cars or traveling through predominantly white neighborhoods. Statistics lend support to these charges. The American Civil Liberties Union reports that blacks comprised 72 percent of the drivers pulled over on a Maryland interstate in the late 1990s, even though they represented only 14 percent of all drivers on that freeway. Similarly, the New Jersey Attorney General maintains that 77 percent of the drivers stopped and searched by New Jersey state police are black or Hispanic— yet only 13.5 percent of motorists on that state's highways are black or Hispanic.

Many commentators point out that these statistics are the result of racial profiling—the use of race as a factor in identifying potential criminal suspects. Police who disproportionately stop and search blacks and Latinos, analysts often argue, are operating on the biased notion that minorities are more likely than whites to carry illegal drugs or be involved in other criminal activity. Critics maintain that this constant scrutiny of minorities is a form of discrimination. While being searched by police may not typically result in arrests, minorities tend to find such investigations humiliating, emotionally draining—and even life-threatening. During the late 1990s, several questionable shootings of black men by police led to speculation about racism in the criminal justice system and whether law enforcement could be trusted to treat minorities fairly. In one 1999 incident in New York City, for example, unarmed African immigrant Amadou Diallo was killed after being shot nineteen times by four white police officers. The officers, who had been searching for a black suspect in a rape case, claimed they shot Diallo after confronting him because he reached into his pocket for his wallet—which they presumed was a gun. The Diallo incident convinced many that racial profiling was a potentially dangerous form of discrimination that needed to be eliminated.

Not everyone believes that racial profiling is unwarranted, however. Some social analysts contend that police officers target minorities simply because they have a higher incidence of criminal activity. According to *U.S. News & World Report*, African Americans compose only 13 percent of the U.S. population but make up 35 percent of all drug arrests and 55 percent of all drug convictions. Moreover, reports journalist William Tucker, blacks commit 46 percent of all robberies and 21 percent of rapes. While the murder rate for whites in 1999 was 3.5 per 100,000, Tucker notes, the rate among blacks was 25.5 per 100,000—seven times the white rate. Given these statistics, he argues, police should not be accused of undue bias when they pursue blacks and Latinos as possible criminal suspects. *National Review* commentator John Derbyshire agrees, explaining that "a policeman who concentrates a disproportionate amount of his limited time and resources on young black men is going to uncover far more crimes—and therefore be far more successful in his career—than one who biases his attention toward, say, middle-aged Asian women." As long as race is just one factor in a generalized approach to finding suspects, Derbyshire writes, it should be taken into account. Similarly, while Tucker grants that racial profiling "undeniably visits indignity on the innocent," he believes that banning it would only undermine the efficiency of police work.

Some critics of racial profiling question the statistics that lead commentators such as Derbyshire and Tucker to conclude that minorities commit a relatively high number of crimes. For example, researcher John Lamberth discovered that among drivers and passengers searched in Maryland, "about 28 percent have contraband, whether they are black or white. The same percentage of contraband is found no matter the race." However, since blacks are three to four times more likely to be searched than are whites, blacks *appear to* have contraband more often than whites. As Lamberth explains, "The data show that for every 1,000 searches by the Maryland State Police, 200 blacks and only 80 nonblacks are arrested. This could lead one to believe that more blacks are breaking the law—until you know that the sample is deeply skewed. Of those searched, 713 were black and only 287 were nonblack." If the justification for racial profiling is rooted in conclusions drawn from misleading data, Lamberth maintains, profiling is patently discriminatory and unfair.

In 1999, federal law enforcement agencies began gathering information about their own police procedures to help determine if they were engaging in discriminatory forms of racial profiling. Since then, several cities and states have begun requiring authorities to keep statistics on the issue, and racial profiling is likely to remain controversial as more data is collected and interpreted.

Racial profiling is just one of the topics at debate within the larger public discussion about discrimination today. The question of whether affirmative action hinders or causes discrimination—and whether multiculturalism and diversity programs curb bias at schools and in the workplace—are also included among the contentious issues considered in this anthology. *Discrimination: Opposing Viewpoints* spotlights these ongoing controversies in the following chapters: Is Discrimination a Serious Problem? Are Claims of Reverse Discrimination Valid? Is Affirmative Action an Effective Remedy for Discrimination? How Can Society End Discrimination? The authors in this volume probe the question of whether all citizens share the same rights, freedoms, and opportunities.

# CHAPTER 1

# Is Discrimination a Serious Problem?

# Chapter Preface

Patricia Flores is a Latina in her late twenties who lives in Seattle, Washington. When *Washington Post* staff writer Michael H. Cottman asked her to describe an experience with intolerance, she recalled several incidents from the year 2000: "I was the first person in the department [store] and not one salesperson spoke to me. But when several white customers walked in, they asked them if they needed any help. . . . Many of my minority friends have had similar experiences. Once I had to get ugly and tell the salesperson that I was next in line, but I don't feel like doing that every time I'm in the store. It makes me feel angry and I decided to shop online and in catalogs because I don't like being treated this way. It's not worth ruining your day."

Whites are often at a loss when they hear of minorities' complaints about discrimination because they may not believe that racial stereotypes influence their own interactions with people of color. Surveys taken in the late 1990s, for example, reveal that 85 to 90 percent of whites claim that they do not harbor any racial prejudices. Some whites maintain that minorities misinterpret relatively harmless incidents, such as being treated rudely by salesclerks or taxi drivers, as examples of discrimination. Since whites themselves encounter rude behavior from other whites in public settings, they might conclude that people of color are simply mistaking unmannerly behavior for racism. Many minorities, however, contend that incidents such as Flores's experience in the department store are not innocuous; nor are they usually the result of misperception. "These are precisely the kinds of incidents that contribute to . . . [minority] middle-class rage—the steady occurrence of slights and put-downs you know in your gut are tied to race but that rarely take the form of blatant racism," claims Harvard Afro-American studies professor Lawrence Bobo. "No one uses the N-word. There is not a flat denial of service. It is insidious, recurrent, lesser treatment."

Some minorities, on the other hand, assert that such occurrences of discrimination should be seen in a different light. Although they grant that racial discrimination still occurs, it is a far cry from the legalized segregation, widespread voter disfranchisement, and blatant denial of opportunity that was typical before the passage of the Civil Rights Act of 1964. It is important, for example, to recognize the progress that has made it possible for minorities to climb the corporate ladder or become elected officials. Black columnist William Raspberry maintains that "the victims of racial, gender, or other injustices might find it useful to keep those injustices in perspective—to separate the major from the minor, the urgent from the merely annoying—in order to put the most effort where it is likely to do the most good."

The pervasiveness and seriousness of racial discrimination is just one of the issues debated in the following chapter. Journalists, scholars, and entrepreneurs also examine claims of discrimination against women and homosexuals.

> "*Racial profiling is only one of many examples of intolerance that minorities say they continue to confront.*"

# Racial Discrimination Is Commonplace

Richard Morin and Michael H. Cottman

Minorities continue to face racial prejudice and discrimination, write Richard Morin and Michael H. Cottman in the following viewpoint. A majority of African Americans, Latinos, and Asians contend that they occasionally encounter racial slurs, poor service, fearful reactions, and disrespectful treatment. In addition, significant numbers of racial minorities claim that they have experienced job discrimination and racially motivated police stops. Most of these charges of discrimination and racial profiling do not stem from minority exaggerations or misperceptions, the authors point out, but instead reflect the truth about continuing racial intolerance. Morin and Cottman are staff writers for the *Washington Post*.

As you read, consider the following questions:

1. According to the authors, what percentage of black men claim that they have been unfairly stopped by police because of their race?
2. What percentage of Latinos and Asians say that they occasionally encounter racial intolerance, according to the survey cited by Morin and Cottman?
3. What percentage of whites report experiencing discrimination within the past ten years, according to the authors?

More than half of all black men report that they have been the victims of racial profiling by police, according to a survey by the *Washington Post*, the Henry J. Kaiser Family Foundation and Harvard University.

Overall, nearly 4 in 10 blacks—37 percent—said they had been unfairly stopped by police because they were black, including 52 percent of all black men and 25 percent of all black women.

Blacks are not the only Americans who say they have been the targets of racial or ethnic profiling by law enforcement. One in five Latino and Asian men reported they had been the victims of racially motivated police stops.

## Continuing Intolerance

But racial profiling is only one of many examples of intolerance that minorities say they continue to confront. More than a third of all blacks interviewed said they had been rejected for a job or failed to win a promotion because of their race. One in five Latinos and Asians also said they had been discriminated against in the workplace because of their race or ethnicity.

Overwhelming majorities of blacks, Latinos and Asians also report they occasionally experience at least one of the following expressions of prejudice: poor service in stores or restaurants, disparaging comments, and encounters with people who clearly are frightened or suspicious of them because of their race or ethnicity.

"These are precisely the kinds of incidents that contribute to what is coming to be called black middle-class rage—the steady occurrence of slights and put-downs you know in your gut are tied to race but that rarely take the form of blatant racism," says Lawrence Bobo, a professor of Afro-American studies and sociology at Harvard University. "No one uses the N-word. There is not a flat denial of service. It is insidious, recurrent, lesser treatment."

A much smaller proportion of whites also say they have been victims of discrimination: One out of every three reported that they sometimes face racial slurs, bad service or disrespectful behavior.

Claims and counterclaims about the prevalence of racial

profiling have been made for years. But there have been few reliable attempts to estimate the degree to which blacks, Latinos and Asians believe they have been victims of the practice. And no national data exist that firmly document the pervasiveness of the practice, making it impossible to compare perceptions with actual incidence.

For this survey, the latest in a series of polls on public policy issues conducted by the *Washington Post*, the Henry J. Kaiser Family Foundation and Harvard University researchers, 1,709 randomly selected adults were interviewed by telephone from March 8 through April 22, 2001. The sample included 315 Hispanics, 323 blacks and 254 Asians.

The margin of sampling error for the overall results is plus or minus 3 percentage points. It is plus or minus 6 points for blacks, 7 points for Latinos and 9 points for Asians.

Widely publicized incidents around the country have drawn attention to the targeting of minorities by police, a practice some police officials have tried to justify by arguing that minorities are more likely to commit crimes. President George W. Bush told Congress in February 2001 that "it is wrong, and we must end it." Democratic Sen. Russell Feingold of Wisconsin and Democratic Rep. John Conyers Jr. of Michigan recently introduced companion bills in the Senate and the House that would withhold funding from agencies that engage in racial profiling.

And suddenly, from New Jersey to California, victims of unwarranted police stops and harassment are telling their stories and, for the first time, are being heard.

## Racial Profiling

Kinte Cutino, 24, a house painter in New Haven, Conn., said he was riding his bike when a police officer pulled him over. "He asked where I was headed, and I told him. He searched me, and didn't find anything and then he let me go."

Cutino shrugged off the encounter. "They will stop you in certain areas, and if you're black, most likely you will get stopped," he said. "You can't do anything about it. That's just the way it is."

Tommy Thorne would seem to be an unlikely target of police attention. Thorne, 62, is a retired Army lieutenant colonel who recently retired as director of an engineering company in Portland, Ore.

But in the year 2000, he and his wife were driving through the Mojave Desert on a vacation trip to Las Vegas. When he pulled his Cadillac Eldorado out of a gas station, "a police car was on my bumper; he was real close. When I turned, he turned; when I changed lanes, he changed lanes. He kept following me.

"Finally I pulled over and waited five minutes. And he stopped. When I pulled off, he followed me again and then came barreling up alongside me and started pulling ahead of me, and backing off, and pulling ahead."

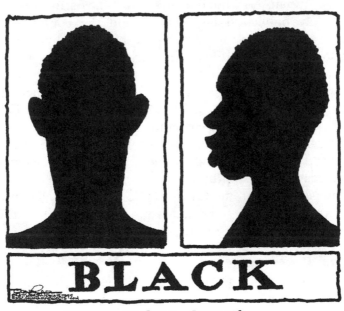

THE COLOR OF RACIAL PROFILING

Conrad. © 1999 by Tribune Media Services, Inc. Reprinted with permission.

Thorne says the officer's intimidating behavior continued for several more miles, and then the officer backed off. "He never pulled me over or issued a summons. It just irritated me. And there was nothing I could do about it. I think he saw a black guy in the desert and thought I was a drug dealer.

Who knows? But I guess if you're black and male, at some point it's going to happen to you."

Steve Jaime, a guest services manager at a suburban Chicago hotel, recalls the night that he and some friends were coming home from the Taste of Chicago food festival when the police stopped their car in a predominantly Hispanic neighborhood. Without explanation, the officers ordered them out of their car.

"That's when the police officer put a gun to my head while he was checking me out," said Jaime, who is Mexican American. Then the officers abruptly told Jaime and his friends to go. "They were pissed off about something and they took it out on us, because we were Hispanic."

## Other Incidents of Racism

The survey found that other forms of racial intolerance are commonplace. More than 8 in 10 blacks and two-thirds of all Latinos and Asians say they occasionally experience at least one of these four intolerant acts: poor service, racial slurs, fearful or defensive behavior, and lack of respect. Two-thirds of all blacks and nearly half of all Latinos and Asians say they experience two or more of these forms of intolerance from time to time.

Sometimes these ugly moments provoke anger, as when a waiter in an expensive steakhouse asked Earl Arredondo, a 30-year-old Latino from Harlingen, Tex., if he could afford the $32 rib-eye steak he had just ordered and later dismissively asked him if he knew "what calamari is."

And sometimes they provoke fear, as when a carload of drunken whites pulled to a stop alongside Martha Matsuoka, an Asian American who lives in Los Angeles. Then they threw beer bottles at her and demanded that she "go home" and "buy American."

"I understand these kinds of things rationally, but personally I was stunned," says Matsuoka, 39, a graduate student at the University of California at Los Angeles. "It was so real. On a personal level, my mother was upset. She said she had hoped that I would never have to experience anything like that."

The prejudice reflected in these incidents is clear. In other instances, perceptions may not reflect reality: An honest error or an unintended slight may be misconstrued as an act of racial intolerance.

But Harvard's Bobo cautions that it would be dangerous to dismiss the bulk of these claims as misperceptions or mis-understandings. "These feelings of victimization are not ar-rived at easily, or because they are pleasant feelings to hold," he said. "We have to regard them as indicators of a very real social phenomenon. For example, blacks complained for years that they were being targeted by police and were ig-nored. Only finally, when a cannon-load of data was shot across the bow, did people begin to say, 'Oh, yeah, I guess it's going on.'"

## Discrimination

Blacks confront far more discrimination than either Latinos or Asians, the survey found. And black men report facing prejudice more often than black women. Nearly half—46 percent—of all blacks said they had experienced discrimina-tion in the past 10 years, including 55 percent of black men and 40 percent of black women.

In 1999, says Ali Barr, a television engineer in Atlanta, he was in Baltimore on business and went to a jazz bar and restaurant with friends to get something to eat.

"It was a white bar, but it featured a black jazz band," Barr says. "But from the moment we walked in, we could feel the hostility. All the patrons were white. The waitress comes over and tells us we couldn't sit in the section we were in. She said it was closed until later in the evening."

"But there were only 10 people in the bar, so we moved to the other section and we asked for coffee. She came back and slammed the coffee down and came back with the manager. The manager said we were not welcome here and that our money wouldn't be accepted."

"The manager pointed to a sign saying that management reserved the right to serve who they wanted. We were asked to leave. All we wanted was something to eat. We were to-tally discriminated against. That will always be my memory of downtown Baltimore."

Four in 10 Latinos and Asians reported that they, too, had been discriminated against in the past 10 years.

Laticia Villegas, 27, owns a children's clothing store in Fort Worth. She recently tried to write a check at a supermarket. The white clerk refused to let her borrow or even touch her pen. Villegas fished around in her purse and wrote the check.

"It is culture shock," Villegas says. "I've never been discriminated against until I moved to Dallas [from San Antonio]. I was offended and surprised; I didn't expect it. I'm not used to being treated this way. I thought we got past this, but we haven't, and I know my [1-year-old] daughter will have to grow up experiencing these kinds of things because she does not have blond hair and blue eyes."

## Anti-White Racism

About 1 in 5 whites—18 percent—also report being the victims of discrimination in the past 10 years. Ten percent said they had been denied a promotion because of their race or ethnicity, 14 percent said they had received poor service because of their race, and an equal proportion reported having been called names or insulted.

Rose Evans, 26, of Aurora, Colo., says she has frequently been the target of racially prejudiced comments from Latinos and blacks.

Evans grew up West Denver, a predominantly Mexican American and Asian neighborhood where "I was picked on quite a bit. You know, 'stupid white girl' and worse things in Spanish. But my stepdad is Mexican American, and I learned to let it roll off of me."

Earlier this year, her 9-year-old daughter confronted prejudice. "A group of little black girls at school were picking on her a lot, calling her 'honky' and stuff. She would come home from school crying. I told her to ignore them, they were just ignorant people."

But the bullying continued, and Evans requested a meeting with school officials and the mother of the girl who had been particularly vicious to her daughter.

"The mother became very hostile and started calling me 'white trash' and 'honky' and other stuff," Evans says. "I told her children aren't born ignorant, they are taught it, and I saw where her daughter got it from."

*"The treatment accorded young [black]
males by police officers . . . and others
cannot be attributed to irrational prejudice.
It is more likely the product of rational
discrimination."*

# Some Racial Discrimination Is Justified

Dinesh D'Souza

In the following viewpoint, Dinesh D'Souza argues that racial discrimination is often based on rational or commonplace assumptions about a person's appearance. For example, he argues, cabdrivers who refuse to give rides to young black males may be discriminating not because of bigotry against African Americans but because of a rational fear based on the high percentage of young black criminals. While such rational discrimination should be illegal in the public sector—that is, police should not be allowed to make race-based stops and searches—it should be tolerated in the private sector because individuals are entitled to protect themselves. D'Souza is a media fellow at Stanford University's Hoover Institution and John M. Olin Scholar at the American Enterprise Institute.

As you read, consider the following questions:
1. According to D'Souza, what percentage of black males between the ages of fifteen and thirty-five are in prison, on probation, or on parole? What percentage of white males?
2. In what way do insurance companies engage in rational discrimination, according to the author?
3. Why should police not be allowed to use race in deciding when to stop or search people, in D'Souza's opinion?

From "When Discrimination Makes Sense," by Dinesh D'Souza, *Hoover Digest*, Fall 1999. Copyright © 1999 by the Board of Trustees of Leland Stanford Junior University. Reprinted with permission.

Two Los Angeles police officers were cruising the city's highways when they saw a black man who looked as if he might be a drug dealer. So they pulled over his car, only to discover that their suspect was Christopher Darden, co-prosecutor in the O. J. Simpson trial.

The cops cheerfully waved Darden on, but he was not amused. Speaking at a recent forum in San Francisco, Darden said he found such incidents "demeaning" and "humiliating," and he accused the police of routinely stopping black men in the belief that they are potential criminals. "Just about everyone I know has been stopped—ministers, doctors, lawyers, professional athletes," he said.

Law enforcement officers call "profiling" likely criminals a necessary part of police work, but African Americans call the practice of being pulled over simply because of the color of their skin "driving while black." Cops aren't the only offending group. Many blacks accuse big-city cabdrivers of refusing to pick up young black males, especially at night. African American men also complain that storekeepers follow them around, as if to prevent stealing, and that women who pass them on the street clutch their purses.

## Is Racism Involved?

The American Civil Liberties Union recently released a report that cited mounting evidence of racially motivated police stops. Some members of Congress and state legislators are demanding that the practice be outlawed. Cabdrivers are being fined and even losing their licenses for passing up young black males. Civil rights leaders are calling for much tougher measures to stop what one terms "a shameful resurgence of racism." Yet in these cases, it is not clear that racism is involved. In Washington, D.C., for example, few of the cabdrivers accused of bigotry for passing up young black males are white. Many are immigrants from El Salvador, Nigeria, Pakistan, and the West Indies, and African American cabdrivers apparently act similarly.

At this point, sociologists are prone to launch into tortuous speculations about how historically victimized groups "internalize" their white oppressors' bigotry. But the explanation for the actions of the nonwhite cabdriver can far more simply and plausibly be attributed to two key facts. First, black males are six to ten times more likely to be convicted of violent crimes than white males. Second, more than 25 percent of black males between the ages of fifteen and thirty-five are, at any given time, in prison, on probation, or on parole. (For whites, the comparable figure is about 5 percent.) Far from being a myth, the reality is that young black males are, by far, the most violent group in U.S. society.

## Some Prejudice Is Warranted

Blacks make up approximately 12 per cent of the nation's population. Yet according to the Uniform Crime Reports, published annually by the FBI, blacks account for 39 per cent of those arrested for aggravated assault, 42 per cent of those arrested for weapons possession, 43 per cent of those arrested for rape, 55 per cent of those arrested for murder, and 61 per cent of those arrested for robbery. Even discounting for the possibility of some racial bias in criminal arrests, it seems clear that the average black person is between three and six times as likely to be arrested for a crime as the average white person. . . .

Personally I would be angry and upset if, as a law-abiding person, I were routinely treated as a criminal by taxidrivers, storekeepers, or pedestrians. Yet, equally predictably, taxidrivers, storekeepers, and women who clutch their purses or cross the street will attach little significance to such personal and historical sensitivities. Such people are unlikely to be intimidated by accusations of prejudice. For them, the charges are meaningless, because the prejudice is warranted. In this context, a bigot is simply a sociologist without credentials.

Dinesh D'Souza, *National Review*, October 9, 1995.

These are uncomfortable social facts, but they are facts. Consequently, the treatment accorded young African American males by police officers, cabdrivers, storekeepers, and others cannot be attributed to irrational prejudice. It is more likely the product of rational discrimination. In a situation in which we have limited information about individuals (cabdrivers, for instance, are not in a position to know their clients personally), we must make group judgments based on probability.

The concept of rational discrimination is easier to grasp if we look outside the racial context. Insurance companies, for example, charge teenage boys higher car insurance rates than teenage girls (or older drivers, for that matter). The reason isn't sexism or antimale prejudice; the statistical reality is that, on average, teenage boys are far more likely than teenage girls to bash their cars. So the insurance company is treating groups differently because they behave differently.

Although rational discrimination against African Americans is a social problem, its magnitude should not be exaggerated. Strictly speaking, it makes no sense for a bank manager to refuse to hire a black teller because blacks as a group have a high crime rate; the manager can easily investigate whether this particular African American job seeker has a criminal record. So also mortgage lenders cannot rationally refuse loans to blacks on the grounds that blacks pose a higher repayment risk; again, the lender can look at each applicant's income and credit history.

Still, rational discrimination is a fact of everyday life, and what to do about it poses a genuine public policy problem. Just because discrimination can be rational does not mean it is always moral. Indeed, the rational discrimination of cops, cabdrivers, and storekeepers is very unfair to the law-abiding African American who has done nothing wrong but is treated as a potential criminal. Yet before we approve harsh punishments against those who practice rational discrimination, we should recall that their only offense is using common sense. Shouldn't African Americans who are legitimately outraged at being victimized by discrimination direct their anger not at cabdrivers or police officers but at the black thieves, muggers, and crack dealers who are giving the entire group a bad name?

## Dealing with Discrimination

My solution is that all forms of racial discrimination, including rational discrimination, should be illegal in the public sector. This means that police officers, who are agents of the state, should not be permitted to use race in deciding whether to question potential muggers or stop suspected drug dealers. The reason: We have a constitutional right to be treated equally under the law, meaning the government has no right to discriminate on the basis of race or color.

This point of principle will seem naive to those who ask about its cost in terms of police efficiency. The prudent answer is that there are other (in my view, more important) costs to be weighed. Government-sponsored rational discrimination has the cataclysmic social effect of polarizing African Americans who play by the rules and still cannot avoid being discriminated against. Even law-abiding blacks become enemies of the system because they find themselves treated that way.

In the private sector, we should be more flexible in dealing with rational discrimination. I think the campaign to go after cabdrivers for alleged bigotry is especially foolish. Of course, as a "person of color" myself, I'd be annoyed and indignant if I could not get a taxi. Yet my right to get a cab, which is the right not to be inconvenienced, seems less important than the cabdriver's right to protect his life and property. In cases such as this, it is better for the government to do nothing.

*"It is . . . unreasonable not to acknowledge that in our own time the conditions for [racial] anger have diminished and the conditions for connection have improved."*

# Racial Discrimination Has Diminished

Ward Connerly

In the following viewpoint, Ward Connerly maintains that racial prejudice and discrimination have diminished, particularly since the Civil Rights Act of 1964. Although racism has not disappeared, the continued intermingling of people of various ethnicities has led to increased tolerance and acceptance of differences. Attitudes and policies that emphasize racial classifications and divisions should be abandoned so that this progress can continue, the author asserts. Connerly, a businessman and regent of the University of California, is author of *Creating Equal: My Fight Against Racial Preferences*.

As you read, consider the following questions:
1. What recent personal experience of Connerly's reveals how difficult it can be to "lay down the burden" of race?
2. According to the author, what percentage of American teenagers have at least one close friend of another race?
3. At what point did Connerly begin to feel welcomed by his white in-laws?

From "Laying Down the Burden of Race," by Ward Connerly, *The American Enterprise*, June 2000. Copyright © 2000 by American Enterprise Institute for Public Policy Research. Reprinted with permission.

Not long ago, after I'd given a speech in Hartford, Connecticut, I saw a black man with a determined look on his face working his way toward me through the crowd. I steeled myself for another abrasive encounter of the kind I've come to expect over the past few years. But once this man reached me he stuck out his hand and said thoughtfully, "You know, I was thinking about some of the things you said tonight. It occurred to me that black people have just got to learn to lay down the burden. It's like we grew up carrying a bag filled with heavy weights on our shoulders. We just have to stop totin' that bag."

I agreed with him. I knew as he did exactly what was in this bag: weakness and guilt, anger, and self-hatred.

## Laying Down the Burden of Race

I have made a commitment not to tote racial grievances, because the status of victim is so seductive and so available to anyone with certain facial features or a certain cast to his skin. But laying down these burdens can be tricky, as I was reminded not long after this Connecticut meeting. I had just checked into the St. Francis Hotel in San Francisco to attend an annual dinner as master of ceremonies. After getting to my room, I realized that I'd left my briefcase in the car and started to go back to the hotel parking garage for it. As I was getting off the basement elevator, I ran into a couple of elderly white men who seemed a little disoriented. When they saw me, one of them said, "Excuse me, are you the man who unlocks the meeting room?"

I did an intellectual double-take and then, with my racial hackles rising, answered with as much irritation as I could pack into my voice: "No, I'm not the man who unlocks the rooms."

The two men shrank back and I walked on, fuming to myself about how racial profiling is practiced every day in subtle forms by people who would otherwise piously condemn it in state troopers working the New Jersey Turnpike. As I stalked toward the garage, I didn't feel uplifted by my righteous anger. On the contrary, I felt crushed by it. It was a heavy burden, so heavy, in fact, that I stopped and stood there for a minute, sagging under its weight. Then I tried to see myself through the eyes of the two old men I'd just run into: someone who was black, yes, but more importantly, someone without luggage, striding purposefully out of the elevator as if on a mission, dressed in a semiuniform of blazer and gray slacks.

I turned around and retraced my steps.

"What made you think I was the guy who unlocks the meeting rooms?" I asked when I caught up with them.

"You were dressed a little like a hotel employee, sir," the one who had spoken earlier said in a genuinely deferential way. "Believe me, I meant no insult."

"Well, I hope you'll forgive me for being abrupt," I said, and after a quick handshake I headed back to the garage, feeling immensely relieved.

## Getting Beyond Race

If we are to lay this burden down for good, we must be committed to letting go of racial classifications—not getting beyond race by taking race more into account, as Supreme Court Justice Harry Blackmun disastrously advised, but just getting beyond race period as a foundation for public policy.

Yet, I know that race is a scar in America. I first saw this scar at the beginning of my life in the segregated South. Black people should not deny that this mark exists: it is part of our connection to America. But we should also resist all of those, black and white, who want to rip open that scar and make race a raw and angry wound that continues to define and divide us.

Left to their own devices, I believe, Americans will eventually merge and melt into each other. Throughout our history, there has been a constant intermingling of people—even during the long apartheid of segregation and Jim Crow. It is malicious as well as unreasonable not to acknowledge that in our own time the conditions for anger have diminished and the conditions for connection have improved.

We all know the compelling statistics about the improvements in black life: increased social and vocational mobility, increased personal prestige and political power. But of all the positive data that have accumulated since the Civil Rights Act of 1964—when America finally decided to leave its racial past behind—the finding that gives me most hope is the recent survey showing that nearly 90 percent of all teenagers in America report having at least one close personal friend of another race.

## One Family's Experience

My wife Ilene is white. I have two racially mixed children and three grandchildren, two of whose bloodlines are even more mixed as a result of my son's marriage to a woman of half-Asian descent. So my own personal experience tells me that the passageway to that place where all racial division ends goes directly through the human heart.

Not long ago, Mike Wallace came to California to interview Ilene and me for a segment of *60 Minutes*. He seemed shocked when I told him that race wasn't a big topic in our family. He implied that we were somehow disadvantaging the kids. But Ilene and I decided a long time ago to let our kids find their way in this world without toting the bag of race. They are lucky, of course, to have grown up after the great achievements of the civil rights movement, which changed America's heart as much as its laws. But we have made sure that the central question for our children, since the moment they came into this world, has always been who are you, not what are you. When we ignore appeals to group identity and focus instead on individuals and their individual humanity, we are inviting the principles of justice present since the American founding to come inside our contemporary American homes.

I won't pretend this is always easy. While a senior at college, I fell in love with an effervescent white woman named Ilene. When Ilene's parents first learned how serious we were about each other, they reacted with dismay and spent long hours on the phone trying to keep the relationship from developing further. Hoping for support from my own relatives, I went home one weekend and told Mom (the grandmother who had raised me) about Ilene. She was cold and negative. "Why can't you find yourself a nice colored girl?" she blurted out. I walked out of the house and didn't contact her for a long time afterward.

Ilene and I now felt secretive and embattled. Marrying "outside your race" was no easy decision in 1962. I knew that

Ilene had no qualms about challenging social norms, but I was less sure that she could deal with exclusion by her family, which seemed to me a real possibility. Nonetheless, she said yes when I proposed, and we were married, with no family members present.

---

## The Need to Acknowledge Progress

Some of us [African Americans], I think, fear that to acknowledge progress is to ease the pressure for changes that still cry out to be made. Some reason that progress itself might yet prove illusory, the advances taken away. Some have known too much of estrangement to ever trust fully in acceptance. And some, it must be said, simply dread the loss of a convenient excuse for their own failure to strive. Meaning, of course, the all-powerful and ever-malevolent "white man."

But if there are multiple reasons some African Americans refuse to call advancement by name, there are also multiple penalties. We lose credibility and moral authority. Worse, we cheat ourselves and our children of things our fathers and mothers struggled that we might have. Like joy, and a sense of our own possibilities.

Leonard Pitts, *Miami Herald*, 1999.

---

I called Mom the day after and told her. She apologized for what she'd said earlier. Ilene's parents were not so quick to alter their position. For months, the lines of communication were down. Sometimes I came home from work and found Ilene sitting on the couch crying.

Finally her parents agreed to see her, but not me. I drove her up to their house and waited in the car while she went in. As the hours passed, I seethed. At one point I started the engine and took off, but I didn't know the area and so, after circling the block, came back and parked again. When Ilene finally came out of the house, she just cried for nearly the entire return trip.

Today, people would rush to hold Ilene's parents guilty of racism.

But even when I was smoldering with resentment, I knew it wasn't that simple. These were good people—hard working, serious, upstanding. They were people, moreover, who had produced my wife, a person without a racist bone in her

35

body. In a sense, I could sympathize with my new in-laws: there were no blacks in their daily life, and they lived in a small town where everyone knew everything about everyone else. Our marriage was a leap nothing in her parents' lives had prepared them to take.

But their reaction to me still rankled. After having to wait in the car that afternoon I vowed never to go near their house again.

For a long time we didn't see Ilene's parents. But we did see her Aunt Markeeta and Uncle Glen. They were wonderful people. Glen, dead now, was a salt-of-the-earth type who worked in a sawmill, and Markeeta had a personality as piquant as her name. They integrated us into their circle of friends, who became our friends too. In those healing days, we all functioned as an extended family.

## The Beginning of Racial Reconciliation

If I had to pick the moment when our family problems began to resolve themselves it would be the day our son Marc was born.

Not long after, we were invited to come for a visit. This time I was included in the invitation. I remember sitting stiffly through the event, which had the tone of the recently released film, *Guess Who's Coming to Dinner?* I was supremely uncomfortable, but I also sensed that the fever had broken. And indeed, a peace process was in place. The visits became more frequent. The frigid tolerance gradually thawed into welcome. There was no single dramatic moment that completed the reconciliation; no cathartic conversation in which we all explored our guilt and misconceptions. Instead, we just got on with our lives, nurturing the relationship that had been born along with my son. It grew faster than he did. Within a year we were on our way to becoming what we are now—a close-knit, supportive family. Today, my relationship with my in-laws could not be better. I love them very much, and they let me know that the feeling is mutual.

The moral is clear. Distance exaggerates difference and breeds mistrust; closeness breaks down suspicion and produces connection. My life so far tells me that our future as a nation is with connection.

*"The average wage gap is not proof of widespread discrimination, but of women making [career] choices . . . in a society where the law has granted them equality of opportunity to do so."*

# Women Do Not Face Wage Discrimination

Diana Furchtgott-Roth

Men's average wages are higher than women's, but this discrepancy is not due to antifemale discrimination, argues Diana Furchtgott-Roth in the following viewpoint. Many women earn less than men because they have spent less time in the career track than men have and because they choose professions that pay less than those typically chosen by men. Moreover, women often find jobs that allow them to combine work and family, which usually means that they work fewer hours than men do. When comparing men and women with similar education and experience, however, the so-called "wage gap" disappears, the author points out. Furchtgott-Roth is a resident fellow at the American Enterprise Institute, a conservative think tank. She is also coauthor of *Women's Figures: An Illustrated Guide to the Economic Progress of Women in America.*

As you read, consider the following questions:

1. According to Furchtgott-Roth, how did statisticians arrive at the conclusion that women are paid only 74 cents to a man's dollar?
2. When did women begin to earn more than half of all bachelor's and master's degrees, according to the author?

April 8, 1999, was dubbed Equal Pay Day by the National Committee on Pay Equity, which joined the National Organization for Women and the AFL-CIO to try to persuade the nation that women are paid only 74 cents on a man's dollar. Their organizational literature proposed stunts such as selling hamburgers for $1 to men but for 75 cents to women; selling cookies with one quarter removed; distributing dollar bills with holes in them to reflect the gaps in women's pay; and organizing a New Year's party on April 8 to recognize that women have begun a new year after catching up to men's earnings from 1998. Such claims draw media attention, but do not accurately describe women's compensation in the American workplace.

At about the same time, the AFL-CIO and the Institute for Women's Policy Research (IWPR) released *Equal Pay for Working Families: National and State Data on the Pay Gap and Its Costs*. This report again propounded the fiction that women are paid only 74 cents on a man's dollar in the United States as a whole, and presented data for women's earnings in individual states. In Louisiana, women's earnings are supposedly 67 percent of men's, whereas in the District of Columbia women earn 97 percent of men's wages. In addition, the report looked at the percent of men and women working in different industries, and concluded that "America's working families lose a staggering $200 billion annually to the wage gap."

If these groups are to be believed, then American women are still second-class citizens, as they were before they had the right to vote. But before declaring another crisis, it is worth looking at how these numbers were put together and some of the reasons behind the differences.

## The Numbers Behind the Wage Gap

During the nineteenth century, employers usually operated on the assumption that women in the labor force earned wages that were merely supplemental to household income. This assumption was reflected in women's average earnings, which, according to most historians, were approximately one-third of men's in 1820, rising to approximately 54 percent of men's by the end of the nineteenth century.

Women's average wages continued to rise relative to men's wages during the twentieth century, reaching 74 percent of men's in 1998.

The 74 percent figure is derived by comparing the average median wage of all full-time working men and women. To obtain figures for individual states, average wages of men and women within that state are compared. So older workers are compared to younger, social workers to police officers, and, since full-time means any number of hours above 35 a week (and sometimes fewer), those working 60-hour weeks are compared with those working 35-hour weeks. These estimates fail to consider key factors in determining wages, including education, age, experience, and, perhaps most importantly, consecutive years in the workforce. That is why in states such as Louisiana, where it is less common for women to work, and where they have less education and work experience, the wage gap is wider. In areas where it is more usual for women to work, such as the District of Columbia, the gap is smaller. But this average wage gap, as it is known, says nothing about whether individuals with the same qualifications who are in the same jobs are discriminated against.

When discrimination occurs, and, as readers know all too well, it does occur, our nation has laws to deal with it. We need to focus on individuals rather than averages, and apply the Civil Rights Act and the Equal Pay Act to eradicate cases of discrimination as they occur.

How much less do equally-qualified women make? Surprisingly, given all the misused statistics to the contrary, they make about the same. Economists have long known that the adjusted wage gap between men and women—the difference in wages adjusted for occupation, age, experience, education, and time in the workforce—is far smaller than the average wage gap. Even just adjusting for age removes a lot of the gap: In 1998, according to data published in Employment and Earnings by the Department of Labor, women aged 16 to 24 made 91 percent of what men made.

The wage gap shrinks dramatically when multiple factors are considered. Women with similar levels of education and experience earn as much as their male counterparts. Using data from the National Longitudinal Survey of Youth, economics professor June O'Neill found that, among people ages 27 to 33 who have never had a child, women's earnings are close to 98 percent of men's. Professor O'Neill notes that "when earnings comparisons are restricted to men and women more similar in their experience and life situations, the measured earnings differentials are typically quite small."

## Why Men's and Women's Wages Differ

What about the remaining gap, often referred to as the unexplained statistical residual? Economists Solomon Polachek and Claudia Goldin suggest that different expectations of future employment, or human capital investment, may explain the residual. In other words, since 80 percent of women have children, they may plan their careers accordingly, often seeking employment in fields where job flexibility is high and where job skills will deteriorate at a slower rate. This allows them to move in and out of the workforce with greater ease, or to shift from full-time to part-time work, if they so choose. But job flexibility frequently comes at the cost of lower wages in these fields.

Tenure and experience are two of the most important factors in explaining the wage gap. According to the U.S. Bureau of the Census, women on average spend a far higher percentage of their working years out of the workforce than men. As demonstrated by economists such as Francine Blau, Andrea Beller, David Macpherson and Barry Hirsch, this means that upon returning to the workplace, women will not earn as much as their male or female counterparts who have more uninterrupted experience.

There are reasonable explanations for the differences in average wages between men and women. First, in the 1960s and 1970s women received fewer undergraduate, graduate, and professional degrees than men. It was only in 1982 that women began to earn more than half of B.A. and M.A. degrees, as they continue to do today. In 1970 women earned about 5 percent of all law and business degrees awarded, compared with about 40 percent today. These 1970 graduates are now highly paid professionals at the peak of their earning potential, and many more of them are men than women.

40

Second, many women still choose to major in specialties which pay less. Women get more degrees in public administration and communications and fewer degrees in math and engineering.

Third, many women choose jobs that enable them to better combine work and family, and these pay less than those with rigid or extensive hours. Even in higher-paying professions such as medicine, many women choose to go into pediatrics, psychiatry, and family practice, all lower-paying fields than surgery, which is more demanding in terms of hours.

## Do Employers Discriminate Against Wives and Mothers?

Many studies link increased numbers of children with decreased earnings. Professor Jane Waldfogel of Columbia University compared the gap in wages between men and women with the same education for two groups, mothers and women without children. She found that in 1991, women without children made 95 percent of men's wages, but mothers made 75 percent of men's wages. The difference can be explained by choices of occupations and hours worked, two variables which were not included in her study.

Naturally, there are different explanations for these data. One is that children take time away from women's careers, both in terms of time out of the workforce to bear the children and in terms of time put into work effort afterwards.

A second explanation is that women who qualify for high-paying jobs—who major in business or math, or who go to the trouble of getting professional training, for example— quite naturally choose to work more. With a high-paying career, it is more tempting to delay having children, or have fewer of them, or none at all.

Of course, many people would say that there is a third explanation: employers discriminate against married women. So wives are paid less for the same work or are forced into positions of low pay. But data show that employers do not pay unmarried women less: Why should the employer care if a woman is married? If employers were against marriage, they would pay married men less. But data show that married men are paid more than unmarried men.

If women were systematically discriminated against, as some assert, then some entrepreneur would be able to step forward and take advantage of this. We would see that firms hiring only mothers would make larger profits than others. In the same way, if women were truly paid only 74 cents on a man's dollar, then a firm could fire all its men, replace them with women, and have a cost advantage over rivals. We do not observe this happening.

## The Problem with Comparable Worth

Since average wage gaps occur naturally in labor markets for reasons described above, the only way to get rid of such gaps is to require not equal pay for equal work, but equal pay for different jobs. That is called "comparable worth," and it aims to eradicate differences in pay across male- and female-dominated occupations. In 1999 comparable worth was proposed by President Bill Clinton in his Equal Pay Initiative, by Senator Tom Harkin in his Fair Pay Act, and by Senator Tom Daschle and Representative Rosa DeLauro in their Paycheck Fairness Act.

Under comparable worth plans, a job's worth would be measured by having officials examine working conditions and the knowledge or skill required to perform a task. These officials would then set "wage guidelines" for male- and female-dominated jobs. These criteria not only favor traditionally female occupations over male ones, but favor education and white-collar jobs over manual, blue-collar work. Neither experience nor risk, two factors which increase men's average wages relative to those of women, are included as job-related criteria. And men's jobs are more dangerous—92 percent of workplace deaths are male.

The AFL-CIO/IWPR study calculated the cost of alleged "pay inequity" caused by the predominance of women and men in different occupational categories. The study compared the wages of workers in female-dominated occupations with those in non-female-dominated occupations. The workers had the same sex, age, race, educational level, marital and parental status, and urban/rural status; they lived in the same part of the country and worked the same number of hours; and they worked in firms of the same size in the same industry. The study concluded that women were underpaid by $89 billion per year because of occupational segregation. Without sex, race, marital and parental status, and firm and industry variables, this figure rose to $200 billion per year.

The study boasts an impressive list of variables, but it leaves out two major factors. First, it omits the type of job, saying in a footnote that "no data on the content of the jobs (the skill, effort, and responsibility required by workers who hold them nor the working conditions in which they work) are available" in the data set used. Second, it leaves out the field of education. It is meaningless to say that the earnings of a man or a woman with a B.A. in English should be the same as the earnings of a man or a woman with a B.A. in math. So the study compares workers without regard to education or type of work: secretaries are being compared with loggers, bookkeepers with oil drillers. Such numbers do not present an accurate estimate of wage gaps, and illustrate the difficulties of implementing the comparable worth proposals suggested by legislators.

## Rational Economic Behavior

The so-called "wage gap" between men and women . . . is due not to senseless discrimination. It's caused by statistical differences in age, education, and continuous years in the work force. Because women experience more interruptions in their working careers than do men—usually because of marriage or childbearing—the wages they can command in the market are slightly discounted. That is not unfair; indeed, it is perfectly rational economic behavior on the part of employers concerned about their bottom lines.

Lawrence Reed, *Freeman*, April 1998.

Advocates of comparable worth deny that they support a centrally-planned economy, and say that all they want to do is stop discrimination against women. But a preference for more time at home with less pay and less job advancement over more time at work with more pay and advancement is a legitimate individual choice for women. Similarly, the choice of some men to retire early and forego additional earnings, a continuing trend, does not prove inequality between young and old. Neither of these phenomena is a policy crisis calling for government interference.

## Women's Choices Should Be Honored

One of the greatest harms that feminists have inflicted on American women is to send the message that women are only fulfilled if their salaries are equal to men's, and that a preference for more time at home is somehow flawed. Neither men's nor women's education and job choices prove social inequality.

The main question in the wage gap debate is whether individuals or employers will bear the costs of women's personal choices, such as majoring in subjects which command lower salaries, and taking time off to raise children. The practical consequences of forcing employers to bear these costs include less hiring—fewer jobs and more machines. In an international economy that means more jobs abroad instead of at home. Women's wages made the biggest strides in the 1980s, a time of strong economic growth but one in which the minimum wage shrank in real terms and affirmative action enforcement was not a priority. There are also issues of fairness. Artificial increases in working women's wages at the cost of lower salaries for men, or higher prices in stores, hurt non-working women who rely on men's incomes. And why stop at comparable worth for men's and women's jobs? Why not have it for jobs between blacks and whites, or the disabled and the healthy, or tall and short people?

The average wage gap is not proof of widespread discrimination, but of women making choices about their educational and professional careers in a society where the law has granted them equality of opportunity to do so. Comparable worth promotes a dependence for women, and a reliance on government for protection. Given women's achievements, such dependence is unnecessary. American women enjoy historically unparalleled success and freedom, and the progress they have made in the past half century will continue.

*"Women's earnings are still much lower than men's . . . [because of] the persistence of sex segregation and the legacy of discrimination."*

# Women Continue to Face Wage Discrimination

Ellen Bravo

Some social analysts have recently argued that the "wage gap" between men and women is steadily decreasing and that women no longer face pervasive discrimination in the workforce. In the following viewpoint, Ellen Bravo contends that women continue to earn less than men do even when they have the same amount of education, experience, and seniority as their male counterparts. She maintains that when women seem to "choose" lower-paying careers that allow them to combine work and family, they are actually being monetarily penalized for attending to family needs. Furthermore, women tend to be clustered in the lower-paying jobs of various occupations, and they often are kept from advancing by both subtle and overt discrimination. Bravo is co-director of 9to5, National Association of Working Women.

As you read, consider the following questions:
1. According to Bravo, female general surgeons make what percentage of the average male general surgeon's salary?
2. What percentage of the workforce is not covered by the Family and Medical Leave Act, according to the author?
3. In Bravo's opinion, what should women do to fight against discrimination in the workforce?

Oh, the thorny problem of the wage gap—what's the right wing to do? They used to say that women didn't deserve as much money as men. But hey, it's the dawn of the twenty-first century; you can't stand by that outdated notion anymore. So in the name of progress, the right has decided to prove that the gap simply doesn't exist. Select a few statistics here, throw in some rosy predictions there, pin any disparity on the choices women themselves have made, and voilà!—the wage gap disappears.

The arguments against the gap are all set out in *Women's Figures: An Illustrated Guide to the Economic Progress of Women in America,* by Diana Furchtgott-Roth and Christine Stolba, published by the conservative American Enterprise Institute.

## Are Women's Salaries Lower?

The authors maintain that young women without children make almost the same amount as men in their fields. Therefore, wherever women earn less than men, factors other than discrimination are at play. Women "choose" lower-paying jobs because these positions offer "much-needed flexibility." Women earn less because they work fewer hours and take more breaks from work to spend time with their children. And women just haven't been in the workforce long enough to gain the experience necessary to rise to the top. Given the growing array of flexible options at work, the greater number of women in jobs previously dominated by men, and the simple passage of time, those women who want to reach the top will be able to do so. Or so say the wage-gap vaporizers.

First off, let's admit it: there's a tiny bit of truth in their argument. Young women who don't have any children and who are just entering the workforce do earn roughly the same salaries as men in their fields. *Women's Figures* would have you believe that those equal paychecks will last. If only it were so. Wait five or ten years. Even if she doesn't take time off to have a family, and puts in the same amount of "face time," the woman who started out on a par with the guy next to her will have gotten fewer raises, smaller bonuses, and less frequent promotions. It's certainly not because she's less competent. This truth was brought home to professors and administrators at the Massachusetts Institute of Technology recently. The university conducted a pay-equity study that confirmed women professors' gut feeling that they weren't faring as well as their male colleagues. It wasn't that the university offered unequal pay—at least not at first. But over the years, men were offered research grants more often than women, given better teaching assignments, nominated for awards more often. And all of that led to higher salaries. MIT is doing something about the problem, thanks to the establishment of a committee on women faculty. Yet Furchgott-Roth and Stolba want us to think there's no problem, so why remedy the situation?

And what about jobs that aren't quite equal, although the work is at least comparable by anyone's standards? Why do maintenance workers make more than cleaning women? The authors of *Women's Figures* don't have an answer to that, since it's a fact that in *any* job or profession where women concentrate, the salaries are lower than in those where men predominate—even when they're doing virtually the same work.

*Despite the figures in* Women's Figures, *it's hard to find jobs in which women make what men do.*

• The Web is one of the newest industries around. But female Internet technology professionals pull in only 88 percent of what men in the field make. Same job, equal seniority, but the paychecks don't match.

• Women in executive, administrative, and managerial positions earn 68 percent of what their male counterparts bring home.

• Female general surgeons take home 77 percent of the average male general surgeon's salary.

• Overall, women still earn only 76 cents for every dollar a man earns. Part of the reason is the poverty wages many women earn. Twelve percent of women in year-round, full-time jobs earned less than $12,500 in 1998. The figures for women of color are even worse—16 percent of African American women and 24 percent of Latinas had such low earnings. Nevertheless, the wage gap between men and women in the U.S. has decreased—it was 59 cents to a dollar in 1961, when the Census Bureau first began looking at pay equity. But the improvement isn't just because women's wages have gone up; it's also because of a drop in men's earnings. Downsizing and the closing of manufacturing plants have forced men to take lower-paying jobs. Men of color have been particularly hard hit by declining pay.

## Do Women Choose Low-Paying Jobs?

What about Furchtgott-Roth and Stolba's other arguments?

• "Women choose lower-paying jobs because they offer more flexibility." That's really playing fast and loose with statistics and with logic. Women may cheerfully choose to be child care workers, but they hardly choose to live in poverty as a result. And forget about flexibility. Most women can't get time off to care for their families. Half of the workforce—mostly the low-paid half—isn't covered by the Family and Medical Leave Act. And many of those who are covered can't afford time off because it's unpaid. Meanwhile, 80 percent of working-poor mothers have less than one week of sick leave, which they have to use to care for family members as well as themselves.

• "Women work fewer hours and take more time off than men." Furchtgott-Roth and Stolba are right about women making sacrifices to care for their families. The question is, should there be a penalty for that? And if so, how long should it last? One study of professional women showed that years after they had taken an average of only 8.8 months of family leave, they still earned 17 percent less than women who had not taken leave. For lower-wage women, taking time off can have even worse repercussions. It may mean losing a job altogether.

• "Women haven't been in the workforce long enough to earn what men do." Forget it. We've already seen that women make less compared to men as time goes on, not more.

## The Legacy of Discrimination

There are other ways *Women's Figures* flouts both statistics and logic. It argues that the reason women are so underrepresented in many occupations is that those jobs require physical strength and involve great hazards. Yet this hardly explains why women make up a scant 3.4 percent of airline pilots or navigators, 10 percent of engineers, and 27 percent of physicians. Nor does it explain the discrepancy between the wage and the inherent worth of work traditionally done by women. Why do accountants make more than kindergarten teachers when both jobs require equal levels of training?

## "Laborers" vs. "Custodial Workers"

Hazel Dews is slightly embarrassed when you ask about her salary. She pauses and then confesses that after 25 years cleaning the Russell Senate Office Building in Washington five nights a week, she makes barely $22,000 a year. That's not what really bothers her, though. What irks her is that men who do the same job earn $30,000.

The men, she explains, are called "laborers." They can progress five grades. The women, however, are called "custodial workers," which means they can only advance two grades. "But," she protests, "they scrub with a mop and bucket. We scrub with a mop and bucket. They vacuum. We vacuum. They push a trash truck. We push a trash truck. The only thing they do that we don't is run a scrub machine. But that's on wheels, so we could do it too."

More than three decades after the Equal Pay Act of 1963, American women working full time still earn an average of 74 cents for each dollar earned by men, according to a report published jointly by the AFL-CIO and the Institute for Women's Policy Research (IWPR) in Washington. This affects all economic classes, but its impact is strongest on lower-income workers: If men and women were paid equally, more than 50 percent of low-income households across the country—dual-earner as well as single-mother—would rise above the poverty line.

Naomi Barko, *American Prospect*, June 19, 2000.

*The truth is, women's earnings are still much lower than men's—and so low period—for complex reasons, most of which come down to the persistence of sex segregation and the legacy of discrimination.*

• *Sex Segregation.* While there has been growing opportunity in jobs formerly closed to women, most women do the same jobs they've always done, and those jobs pay less than comparable jobs done by men. Even within certain occupations, such as sales, women are clustered in the lower-paying jobs. For instance, women constitute 82 percent of employees in gift and novelty shops but only 19 percent of those in

"The second day of work, they stole my security card and pasted my photo on the head of a man in the middle of this gay threesome," says Mark Anderson, describing the beginning of a train of abuses he suffered as a stockbroker trainee in Los Angeles for Cantor Fitzgerald & Co., the largest government securities trading firm in the world. "Then they put the photo on the bulletin board and said, 'Now we know why Mark Anderson was hired: to service our bisexual clientele.'"

Most Americans would probably find such treatment unfair and offensive. Indeed, polls conducted by the Human Rights Campaign, a national gay lobbying group, indicate that 68% of voters are in favor of federal legislation to protect gays and lesbians from job discrimination. But that doesn't necessarily mean clear sailing for the federal Employment Non-Discrimination Act [ENDA], which was expected to be introduced in the Senate in May 1997. Opponents of the act, rather than appealing to antigay bias, have been trading on the perception that the bill simply isn't needed. [ENDA would prohibit employment discrimination on the basis of sexual orientation. As of 2001, Congress had not passed ENDA.]

Most gays, especially those facing discrimination at work, would certainly disagree. Should it pass in Congress and be signed into law, ENDA will no doubt represent a major victory in the struggle for gay rights. But observers following individual cases of workplace bias say it will be no panacea.

## Employers Skirt Antidiscrimination Laws

Particularly at the state level, where such antidiscrimination laws already exist, employers are finding ways around them. "When there are legal protections prohibiting discrimination in employment, private individuals will often try to interfere with their enforcement," says Amelia Craig, executive director of Gay and Lesbian Advocates and Defenders, a Boston-based legal group.

No one understands that better than Anderson. "I kept hoping I would get through the training portion of it and then all this stuff would stop," he says, referring to coworkers' homophobic epithets and the showers of spitballs and dirty tissues he endured. "So I figured that I would tolerate this garbage for a chance at a career. I didn't realize it was going to be this bad."

A final incident revealed how entrenched the homophobia was at Cantor Fitzgerald. While Anderson was in New York for additional training, Cantor executives shot a video that includes footage of Anderson's car covered with such gay-bashing slogans as POO-STABBER, BUTT PIRATE, and POLE SMOKER. They then allegedly showed the video at a company sales conference, pretending to introduce it as a training tape for brokers seeking business in a gay section of Los Angeles. Knowing nothing about the car or the video, Anderson was in attendance as several hundred people viewed the tape. After the conference the company distributed more than 100 copies of the video to clients, competitors, and others.

It was only after enduring this treatment for 13 months, in 1994 and 1995, that Anderson was fired. In response he filed a suit in California state court. His case is on hold, however, and it's unclear whether it will be heard, since, like all Cantor trainees, Anderson signed a document upon commencing employment stating that he would settle any disputes with the company through arbitration. Cantor officials declined to comment on the case.

## Same-Sex Sexual Harassment

Sometimes the role played by sexual orientation is less clear-cut but no less critical in obstructing a worker's access to justice. Such was the case for Susan Davis, a therapist at Hennepin County Home School, a Minneapolis-area juvenile correctional facility. Davis says that for 2½ years she was sexually harassed by a female coworker and that her boss failed to address the situation simply because it involved two women.

"It started with this coworker of mine that I rented a room to in my house," Davis recalls. "She wanted more out of the situation, but I was already involved with somebody. Within a few months I had to ask her to leave. That's when the workplace stuff started—buying me gifts, cleaning up after me. She would hug and stroke me, tell nasty sexual jokes.

And through all this she would tell other employees that she and I were involved in an intimate sexual relationship."

Davis talked to the coworker's boss and other administrators, she says, but they refused to take the situation seriously. "They never wanted to address the fact that this was a woman harassing another woman," Davis says. Instead they insisted that Davis had brought the situation on herself. A county official did not return phone calls asking for comment.

## Antigay Discrimination in the Workplace

Congress knows how pervasive employment discrimination against gays and lesbians has been and is. And case studies about how many gay men and lesbians have lost or been denied jobs or promotions vastly understate the problem. The threat of discrimination is a very real presence in most American workplaces. For example, a 1987 *Wall Street Journal* poll of Fortune 500 executives showed 66% would hesitate to give a management job to a lesbian or gay man. Most gay men and lesbians attempt to protect themselves against the threat of discrimination by hiding their identity. But hiding one's identity is no simple task. It requires carefully policing even the most casual conversations, and banishing almost any acknowledgment of family and friends from the workplace (those who doubt it should try to see how far they can get through a single day without referring to a spouse or companion). In addition to being difficult to do, hiding one's identity is harmful; it hurts the workplace, building walls between co-workers, and it can impose a terrible psychological toll on those forced to do the hiding.

American Civil Liberties Union, congressional testimony, July 17, 1996.

The harassment began in October 1991; in 1994 Davis filed suit in a case that has now been appealed to the Minnesota supreme court. Although in Davis's view sexual-orientation discrimination was central to her case, in the end that argument appeared too difficult to prove and was dropped from the suit.

## Antidiscrimination Laws Are No Cure-All

Antidiscrimination laws, of course, will not by themselves bring such conflicts to an end. No one could have seemed better protected from antigay bias on the job than Polly

Attwood, a teacher at Brookline High School in Brookline, Mass. With Massachusetts law prohibiting employment discrimination based on sexual orientation and with a nondiscrimination clause in her teaching contract, Attwood felt safe identifying herself as a lesbian in the classroom when it seemed appropriate—for instance, in the course of discussions about state initiatives to protect gay men and lesbians.

Following one such instance, however, a female student and her family expressed to Attwood that they had found the revelation upsetting. The student stopped coming to class and eventually left the school. Almost two years later, in March 1996, the student's parents threatened to sue Attwood and the school for more than $300,000, claiming their daughter had suffered severe emotional distress. Although they never followed through on their threat, it remains a liability hanging over Attwood's head, and some see the threatened lawsuit as part of a trend in strategy for opponents of gay rights.

Such backhanded forms of employment discrimination are just as likely in corporate settings, where conservative workers may level charges that an openly gay colleague has violated their religious rights, predicts Craig. "I could imagine that one might see a dispute by some employee claiming it's not fair to have an out gay employee wearing a pink triangle, for example," she says.

Indeed, such a dispute has led, according to the employees involved, to two dismissals in a case involving AutoNation USA, a Florida-based company that sells used cars. In November 1996, Brian Long, an AutoNation employee in Grapevine, Tex., wrote a letter to the company's chief executive officer expressing concern about the termination of Lyndse Stratton, a temporary employee who was released after a conflict over a gay rights poster she had displayed in her cubicle. Two weeks later—with no response from the CEO—Long, who is gay, posted a copy of the letter to a company computer server, making it accessible to all employees. The following month Long was informed that he was being investigated. A few days later he was fired.

Even though Texas has no law against antigay discrimination, Long says AutoNation officials told him the termination was based on "misuse of the E-mail system": "I was told again and again that it had nothing to do with my sexuality." (AutoNation officials could not be reached for comment.) In fact, Long says, the internal server he used to transmit the document was also used by other staff members for nonwork-related items. Although Long believes antigay discrimination played a role in his termination, he says legal advisers told him that a case citing violation of First Amendment rights would be much stronger than anything related to sexual orientation. In the end he decided he had nothing to gain by pursuing legal redress.

Even as more laws opposing it are written, employment discrimination related to sexual orientation may become harder to prove, says Jon Davidson, a supervising attorney with Lambda Legal Defense and Education Fund in Los Angeles. "As with any area of discrimination, the first cases that you see are the most blatant ones," Davidson says. "Once employers become more sophisticated, the discrimination doesn't automatically go away, but it does tend to be more hidden."

That doesn't mean, of course, that laws like ENDA are ineffective—or unnecessary. "Whatever laws are there, some employers will try to get around them," says Davidson. Others, however, will be deterred from discriminating in the first place. That's a benefit that's hard to measure, but worthwhile.

*"Homosexuals as an entire class are not disadvantaged, possess no inborn, obvious or unchangeable characteristics—and certainly are not politically powerless."*

# Homosexuals Do Not Face Significant Discrimination

Concerned Women for America

Homosexuals are not a disadvantaged minority group, argues Concerned Women for America (CWA) in the following viewpoint. Although homosexual activists often claim that they face discrimination, homosexuals as a group have not exhibited an inability to obtain income, education, or political power because of prejudice against their sexual practices. Furthermore, CWA maintains, homosexuality is not an unchangeable characteristic, such as race or gender, that sets a group apart as a discrete class in need of protection from discrimination. Ultimately, "gay rights" antidiscrimination ordinances can infringe on the rights of employers, schools, and organizations that disapprove of the homosexual lifestyle. CWA is a national organization that promotes traditional Judeo-Christian values.

As you read, consider the following questions:
1. According to CWA, why is Alveda King insulted by the homosexual community's attempts to be granted protected class status?
2. What is the average household income of homosexuals, according to the authors?
3. In the opinion of CWA, how would protected class status for homosexuals set "a frightening precedent"?

Homosexual extremists wish to be granted protected class status—special legal standing and advantages historically applied by governments in the United States to classes of people characterized as distinct and unchanging in status.

Countless studies consistently show that homosexuals as an entire class are not disadvantaged, possess no inborn, obvious or unchangeable characteristics—and certainly are not politically powerless.

If homosexuals are not models of a disadvantaged minority class, then what? Disregarding the standard "gay rights" rhetoric, a look at the facts reveals the plain truth. The "gay rights" movement is nothing more than a powerful special interest lobby. This group is intent on using its money and political influence to "piggyback" on the legitimate gains of the disadvantaged. They strive to gain special rights and privileges at the expense of others truly in need.

## Behavior Does Not a Minority Make

Alveda King, Martin Luther King Jr.'s niece, who is founder and chairman of King for America, is insulted by the homosexual community's attempts to equate their crusade for special rights with the civil rights movement led by Dr. King. Race is a benign and immutable characteristic—homosexuality is a behavior that can be changed. Miss King spoke in a press conference in response to the California initiative that would give homosexuals protected status:

> I used to be very overweight. When I was large, I could have chosen to be a victim, like many other obese people, and lobbied for laws protecting obese people from discrimination, but [instead] I decided to make a change. That's what we're facing today in the debate over homosexual rights. Homosexuals can either choose to be victims, or choose to make a change.

Essentially, homosexuals, bisexuals and lesbians—by their own admission—share only one attribute on which they base their claim to protected class status: They choose to perform sexual acts with members of the same sex. But behavior alone is not a compelling reason to reward protected, minority or ethnic class status with all the attendant entitlements.

The U.S. Supreme Court has declared that not all forms

of sexual behavior, even sexual acts between "consenting adults," are immune from legal regulation or penalty. Incest, pedophilia and prostitution are but a few examples of behavior considered criminal acts by legal statutes.

Therefore, the question homosexual extremists raise is this: Should behavior alone compel federal, state and local governments to grant homosexuals legally sanctioned "protected class" status with all the accompanying special entitlements and privileges?

## Homosexuals Demand Special Rights

Concerned Women for America does not question homosexuals' claim to legal protection shared by all citizens on condition of good behavior. However, available information about homosexual behavior and the current economic, cultural and political status of homosexuals in our society discredit the need for homosexuals to qualify for special protected class status.

Historically, protected class status is determined by the courts and civil rights authorities by three standards. They are:

- As an entire class, they have suffered a history of discrimination evidenced by lack of ability to obtain economic income, adequate education or cultural opportunity.
- As an entire class, they exhibit obvious, immutable or distinguishing characteristics, such as race, color, gender [male or female] or national origin that define them as a discrete group.
- As an entire class, they clearly demonstrate political powerlessness.

The question must then be asked: Based on these standards, do homosexuals qualify as a protected minority?

## A Look at the Three Standards

*Standard #1: A history of discrimination evidenced by lack of ability to succeed.* Homosexuals are enormously advantaged relative to the general population. A flier from the Institute for International Research in New York City quoted a survey conducted by Simmons Market Research Bureau which claims that homosexuals have an average household income of $63,100 versus a general population income of $36,500.

By contrast, the average income of a disadvantaged African-American household is somewhere between $12–13,000.

*Standard #2: Specially protected classes should exhibit obvious, immutable or distinguishing characteristics, like race, color, gender [male or female] or national origin.* Although there have been newspaper articles reporting "breakthrough evidence" claiming homosexuality to be genetic, there is no credible evidence to support the claims that "gayness" is either genetically determined or unchangeable. In the journal *Science*, a team from the University of Western Ontario conducted a study of possible genetic links to homosexuality and concluded, "Our data does not support the presence of a gene of large effect influencing sexual orientation." Not only is the weight of scientific evidence to the contrary, but there are innumerable cases of "ex-gay" individuals. Across the nation, organizations that specialize in reparative therapy can attest to the fact that men and women are leaving the "gay" lifestyle.

*Standard #3: Specially protected classes should clearly demonstrate political powerlessness.* During the 1996 elections, the Human Rights Campaign Fund, a homosexual political advocacy group, raised more than $1.4 million. This put it in the top one percent of political action committees (PACs) nationwide.

With gay and lesbian leaders meeting with the President in the White House, a gay White House liaison to the homosexual community, and the appointment of lesbian activist Roberta Achtenberg to Assistant Secretary of Fair Housing and Equal Opportunity at the Department of Housing and Urban Development, the argument that homosexuals need protected class status due to political powerlessness is simply not true.

To illustrate the point further that homosexuals as a class are not politically powerless, [former] Vice President Al Gore wrote in a letter to one of CWA's members:

> This Administration has taken more steps than any previous to bring the gay and lesbian communities to the table. We have more openly gay and lesbian individuals serving in appointed positions, and their impact—through both their expertise and their efforts to advocate for the concerns of gay and lesbian Americans—has been significant.

In other words, homosexuals are upwardly mobile, politically powerful citizens who have chosen to involve themselves in sexual behavior that is neither inborn nor unchangeable. Now, they are clamoring for protected class status—special legal standing and advantages historically applied by governments in the United States to classes of people sharing distinct and immutable characteristics.

## What Will They Cost Us?

Society has seen fit to withhold its blessing and special protection from other shared behaviors—murder, theft and fraud, and "sexual orientations" like necrophilia, bestiality and pedophilia. When people act out these behaviors, society reacts with revulsion and punishment. These "orientations" obviously represent a clear and present danger to the physical, mental, cultural and spiritual health of the citizenry. Protected class status bestowed on homosexuals as an entire class would represent the first awarding of such status based solely on behavior—a frightening precedent.

---

### Homosexuals Rarely Face Discrimination

In spite of the fact that individual homosexuals sometimes face reprehensible behavior from roughnecks and bullies, as a group they are far from "oppressed." On the contrary, as a group, white homosexuals have always enjoyed their full constitutional rights. This is demonstrated by the fact that they enjoy higher than average incomes than most Americans, and they are more likely to hold advanced college degrees and more prestigious occupations than any other group.

In actuality, homosexuals are rarely discriminated against in the job market or when seeking housing, in spite of their anecdotal stories to the contrary. In most places, they have reputations as reliable workers and good rent-paying tenants. But the concept of "discrimination," which associates them with blacks and other "downtrodden" unfortunates, is a powerful one, guaranteed to arouse public sympathy.

Elizabeth Wright, *Issues and Views*, Spring 1996.

---

The special homosexual rights ordinances that have sprung up around the country encroach upon the rights of ordinary citizens. Bills prohibiting discrimination based upon sexual orientation and acts pertaining to hate crimes sharply limit the rights of the American people. They interfere with businessmen's rights to direct the affairs of their companies, school districts and youth organizations. They interfere with their right to hire men and women with sound moral principles to teach our children. Moreover, the bills threaten the First Amendment rights of pastors to preach against homosexuality. They also curtail speech and freedom of conscience. When citizens are forced to undergo mandatory "sensitivity training" courses in the federal and private workplace, gay "rights" ordinances threaten the right of:

- Schools to hire teachers of high moral caliber
- Parents and school districts to protect students from homosexual curriculum and recruitment by homosexual "counseling" groups
- Pastors to preach against the sin of homosexuality
- Employers to determine if a person's moral standing will interfere with his/her work place duties
- Employees to express their disapproval of the homosexual lifestyle
- Communities to deny special protection to behavior that has a negative impact upon public health. (The CDC reports that the homosexual population has the highest incidence of HIV and AIDS.)

We must remember that it was a sexual orientation non-discrimination bill that opened the door for homosexuals to sue for the right to marry in Hawaii. Currently, the Vermont Supreme Court is considering the case *Baker vs. State of Vermont* in which one homosexual couple and two lesbian couples filed suit to legalize same-sex marriage. In Hawaii and Alaska, voters overruled the courts in statewide referenda. However, Vermont has no state referenda. [In December 2000, the Vermont Supreme Court ruled that the state must grant the same protection to gay couples as it does to married couples.] The people would have to amend the state constitution, which is not possible until 2002. Approval by the court would also provide a means of overturning the Defense of Marriage Act (DOMA). [DOMA forbids federal recognition of same-sex marriages and gives states the right to refuse to recognize gay marriages performed in other states.]

Same-sex unions, marriage to a minor, bestiality—as well

as polygamy—have all been proscribed by law, because they are harmful to the health and moral welfare of society. Likewise, sodomy has traditionally been prohibited, because it is harmful not only to society, but also to the men and women who engage in it. Diseases range from STDs to hepatitis B, gay bowel syndrome, bacterial infections, to the highest incidence of AIDS. It is clear that society cannot condone such behavior.

## Just Say "No" to Special Rights

It's time to stand up to the onslaught against traditional values in this country. The truth of the matter is that homosexuality is an immoral behavior that can be changed. Under no circumstances should it be given society's stamp of approval.

Homosexual "rights" are not about equality under the law, which gays already possess, but about *special privileges*. Sexual behavior never warrants special protected class status. If given that privilege, our right to hold moral and spiritual standards will be violated. Essentially, our culture will be legislatively mandated.

# Periodical Bibliography

The following articles have been selected to supplement the diverse views presented in this chapter.

Naomi Barko "The Other Gender Gap," *American Prospect*, June 19, 2000.

James H. Carr "The Complexity of Segregation: Why It Continues," *Vital Speeches*, August 1, 1998.

Darryl Fears "From the 'Driving While Black' Files," *Washington Post National Weekly Edition*, November 22, 1999.

David Gelernter "Gay Rights and Wrongs," *Wall Street Journal*, August 13, 1998.

Al Gini "Women in the Workplace," *Business and Society Review*, no. 99, 1998.

Wendy Kaminer "Bigots' Rights," *American Prospect*, June 19, 2000.

Susan Katz Keating "They Had a Dream," *American Legion Magazine*, September 1998.

John Leo "Gender Wars Redux," *U.S. News & World Report*, February 22, 1999.

Malik Miah "Racism and the Wealth Gap," *Against the Current*, September/October 2000.

Philip Perlmutter "The Semantics and Politics of Bigotry," *American Outlook*, Winter 2000.

William Raspberry "'Nothing's Changed?'" *Washington Post National Weekly Edition*, March 9, 1998.

Gabriel Rotello "Gay and Lesbian Rights," *Social Policy*, Spring 1998.

Bertram Rothschild "Computing Gender Bias," *Humanist*, March 2000.

Christina Hoff Sommers "The 'Fragile American Girl' Myth," *American Enterprise*, May/June 1997.

Helen Thomas "Racism Is Alive and Well," *Liberal Opinion Week*, September 10, 2001.

Woody West "Confronting the Profiling Bogeyman," *Insight*, April 2–9, 2001.

# CHAPTER 2

# Are Claims of Reverse Discrimination Valid?

# Chapter Preface

Efforts to reduce discrimination and foster acceptance of diversity include the use of school curricula and educational programs that emphasize America's multicultural nature. Many educators argue that it is imperative for today's students to learn to function in culturally diverse environments because the nation's population is changing—after 2010, for example, several states and urban areas will no longer have a "majority" ethnic group—that is, a racial group that comprises more than 50 percent of the population. One goal of multicultural education is to increase students' awareness of the histories and traditions of America's many racial and ethnic groups. Critics, however, contend that multicultural education is often divisive because it de-emphasizes Americans' common heritage and engenders discrimination against whites.

Supporters of multicultural education contend that minority perspectives have often been excluded from the study of history, literature, and the humanities. Such exclusion can lead students to conclude that civilization is solely the product of European males and their white descendants. This ignorance of the multiethnic nature of history intensifies intolerance and stifles moral and intellectual development, multiculturalists argue. The purposeful inclusion of minority and female viewpoints in school curricula, they maintain, helps students to broaden their perspectives and, ultimately, contribute to the common good. According to educator James A. Banks, multicultural education "helps students transcend their cultural boundaries and acquire the knowledge, attitudes, and skills needed to engage in public discourse with people who differ from themselves and to participate in the creation of a civic culture."

Critics argue that while the stated goals of multicultural education are laudable, the methods that some multicultural educators use amount to reverse discrimination because they unfairly induce guilt in white students. Conservative columnist Paul Craig Roberts claims that "halls of learning have become reeducation camps, where legions of 'diversity educators' and 'sensitivity experts' strive to 'get inside' the minds of white students and replace private conscience, identity and belief with group guilt. Propaganda and emotional manipulation are used to teach whites to think the best about 'people of color' and the worst about themselves." Analyst Alvin J. Schmidt agrees, contending that multiculturalist textbooks tend to ignore the negative aspects of minority histories while maligning or omitting the positive achievements of Euro-American culture. "If [multiculturalists] were truly interested in teaching students about all cultures," states Schmidt, "they not only would include negative incidents of non-Western cultures, but would also note how Western and American culture eliminated unjust practices such as slavery." Such a distorted portrayal of history, he asserts, is a form of antiwhite discrimination that ultimately thwarts the goal of education.

Claims of reverse discrimination on campus, in the workforce, and in society at large continue to provoke heated debate. The viewpoints in the following chapter offer further exploration of this controversy.

*"Affirmative action is . . . a powerful engine for perpetuating preferential treatment and discrimination based on race, sex, ethnic origin, or some other approved badge of victim status."*

# Affirmative Action Creates Reverse Discrimination

*New Criterion*

Affirmative action policies are intended to ensure equal opportunities for minorities and women. However, argue the editors of the *New Criterion* in the following viewpoint, affirmative action actually creates reverse discrimination by requiring the preferential treatment of minorities in hiring and in college admissions. To support their assertion, the authors examine the policy at the University of Michigan, wherein minority students are granted an extra twenty points toward admission simply because of their ethnic origin. Such policies discriminate against whites and breed cynicism and resentment, the authors conclude. The *New Criterion* is a monthly journal of conservative opinion.

As you read, consider the following questions:
1. According to the authors, in what way is affirmative action a form of "doublethink"?
2. How many points do applicants to the University of Michigan receive for outstanding personal achievement, according to the *New Criterion*?
3. In what way did the *Bakke* case of the late 1970s create confusion about quotas, in the authors' view?

From "Notes & Comments: January 2001," *New Criterion*, January 2001. Copyright © 2001 by the Foundation for Cultural Review. Reprinted by permission of New Criterion.

> Doublethink means the power of holding two contradictory beliefs in one's mind simultaneously, and accepting both of them.

— George Orwell, Nineteen Eighty-Four

We have often had occasion to dilate on the Orwellian nature of the phrase "affirmative action" in this space. We are going to do so again. Memories are short; ideological pressure is unremitting; in short, some things cannot be repeated too often. Rhetorically, as we all know, "affirmative action" is redolent of high principle and the struggle for equality. One can almost hear strains of the Marseillaise echoing behind its syllables—or maybe that sound is only the thump of a judge's gavel ordering some new social experiment. In any event, "affirmative action" suggests, . . . well, something good: something positive, something affirmative. (Also, of course, something pragmatic: we're talking about action here, not theorizing: results, not starry-eyed speculation.) And the opponents of affirmative action, what do they want? Something beginning with "N" at any rate: something involving the word "no," something negative, and no doubt impractical to boot.

In actuality, of course, affirmative action is first and foremost a powerful engine for perpetuating preferential treatment and discrimination based on race, sex, ethnic origin, or some other approved badge of victim status. It is not about assuring equality of opportunity but artificially—that is, judicially—enforcing equality of outcome.

It sounds quite different when put like that, doesn't it? But liberals never do put it like that. They love the phrase "affirmative action" precisely because it allows them to avoid acknowledging—perhaps even recognizing—the unpleasant actuality at the heart of affirmative action. This is one reason that connoisseurs of Orwellian obfuscation cannot admire the phrase "affirmative action" too greatly. It is a gift that just keeps on giving. It is vague enough to cover nearly any contingency, pompous enough always to garner partisan support. Talk of "affirmative action" automatically catapults one onto the moral high ground, at least rhetorically, even if it allows one to pursue inequitable programs of social engineering and racial or sexual redress. (Some liberals acknowledge the inequity involved in enforcing the diktats of affirmative-action programs; those who do will generally point out—usually *sotto voce* and with a rueful smile—that one cannot make an omelette without breaking a few eggs.)

## Doublethink in College Admissions

Perhaps the greatest boon conferred by embracing affirmative action is an insensibility to contradiction. It nudges one blissfully over the "hard place" one faces when simultaneously affirming X and not-X. It is an invitation to what Orwell called Doublethink. College admissions are a laboratory case. We all know about the many colleges whose applications begin by declaring that admission will be granted without consideration of race, sex, creed, or national origin—and then go on a few pages later to inform applicants that it is to their advantage if they are black, Hispanic, American Indian, etc., etc. (We have been told, but have not verified, that at least one distinguished university even has a category for "current gender.") "Check here" they say, "and we'll see what we can do for you."

It turns out, of course, that many universities are prepared to do quite a lot for applicants who meet the correct racial/sexual/ethnic profile. Consider the University of Michigan. In December 2000, a federal judge ruled that the two-tiered admission system employed by the university from 1995 to 1998 was unconstitutional because it employed different admission criteria for whites and minorities. It was, plain and simple, a matter of separate but unequal. Well and good, you say: at last a victory in the war against quotas. Not so fast. For in the same ruling, Judge Patrick J. Duggan said that the university's current policy, which automatically awards twenty points (out of a possible 150) to black and Hispanic applicants is just fine. So it is "No" to what Judge Duggan called "fixed racial quotas" but "full steam ahead" when it comes to "consideration of an applicant's race during the admissions process." No wonder he went on to observe that "in situations such as this, it is often a thin line that divides the permissible from the impermissible." So thin, we fear, that one would have to be an affirmative-action activist to be sure of discerning it.

# The Point System

Let's put Michigan's twenty-point bonus into perspective. As the *New York Times* reported on December 14, 2000, applicants can get up to eighty points for their grades. They can get another twelve points for stellar performance on so-called standardized tests ("so-called" because affirmative action has come to the Scholastic Aptitude Tests as well). Being a Michigan resident gets them ten points, being the child of an alumnus four. According to the *Times*, "an outstanding essay, leadership, or personal achievement are each worth 3 points" that is, a mere nine points total for factors that one might have thought should count—that once upon a time in fact did count—a great deal in the admission process. But then what is a terrific essay, outstanding leadership, or superior "personal achievement" in comparison with skin color or (the right) ethnic origin? Not much in Michigan, apparently, for that is all it takes to qualify for the university's twenty-point gift.

## Criticism of Affirmative Action

Affirmative action has replaced discrimination against women and minorities with discrimination against white men—reverse discrimination. Critics of affirmative action argue that while such ideals as equal employment opportunity sound good in principle, in practice they have come to conceal equally unjust, equally harmful, and probably unconstitutional practices that give preference to some at the expense of others.

These practices, critics add, have replaced individual rights with group entitlements, and the concept of equal opportunity with demands for equal outcomes, which in turn have produced quotas in workplace hiring and promoting, in government subcontracting, and in college admissions and faculty hiring. The result has been compromised standards throughout the economy and the educational system. These policies have undermined the long-standing ideal of admitting students to college, hiring and promoting employees, and awarding contracts on the basis of merit rather than politics.

Steven Yates, *Civil Wrongs: What Went Wrong with Affirmative Action,* 1994.

You see the vertiginous land of Oz one enters by embracing affirmative action. But what is a poor judge to do? Back in the late 1970s in the infamous *Bakke* case, the U.S. Supreme Court institutionalized confusion by simultaneously forbidding explicit quotas while upholding the unofficial quotas mandated by the demand for "diversity"—another Orwellian mantra. The Michigan ruling dramatizes that confusion. What it amounts to is a species of racial profiling, though of course we must not call it that. At bottom, affirmative action is the application of welfare mentality to academia and the business world. It is a hand out, not a hand up, and its ultimate effect is to harden the very prejudice it claims to be battling. It creates a two-track system in which some people succeed by dint of hard work, talent, and accomplishment, while others succeed at least partly by dint of racially- or sexually-mandated preferential treatment. Everyone recognizes this, the beneficiaries as well as the victims of affirmative action. The result is an increase in cynicism, resentment, and, not least, the selfish spirit of litigiousness.

Perhaps the most troubling aspect of the Michigan decision is the suggestion that the policies it endorses will have to go on indefinitely. According to Judge Duggan, the University of Michigan's points-for-minorities system is not a temporary expedient but one attempt to address a permanent inequality. "[T]he need for diversity lives on perpetually," he was quoted in the *Times* as saying, and programs to enforce it could therefore continue until the "day when universities are able to achieve the desired diversity without resort to racial preferences." "Perpetually" is a very long time. Today Michigan gives minorities twenty points; maybe it will have to be fifty next year to achieve the same result. George Orwell encapsulated the contradiction inherent in such procedures perfectly when he wrote, in *Animal Farm*, that "all animals are equal, but some animals are more equal than others." There, too, the rhetoric of fairness was employed to institutionalize the reality of inequality.

We observed above that embracing affirmative action tended to impart an insensibility to contradiction. Insensibility, it is worth noting, is not the same as immunity, as those unfortunate people who lack feeling in some part of their body know well. Just because you are without pain does not mean your hand has not been burned.

| "White racism continues to perforate
| equal opportunity."

# Affirmative Action Does Not Create Reverse Discrimination

Part I: William Raspberry; Part II: Derrick Z. Jackson

The authors of the following two-part viewpoint maintain that affirmative action and other policies intended to redress institutionalized racism do not discriminate against whites. In Part I, *Washington Post* columnist William Raspberry argues that people who bemoan so-called reverse discrimination fail to recognize the pervasive racism that minorities face; moreover, they are blind to the inherent privileges granted to whites. In Part II, *Boston Globe* commentator Derrick Z. Jackson contends that critics of affirmative action who support allegedly "color-blind" policies are ignoring the fact that white racism is still a serious problem. Many whites who claim that no one should be judged by their skin color, for example, are unsympathetic to blacks' complaints about being passed up by cabdrivers.

As you read, consider the following questions:

1. According to Raspberry, why did some of his readers resent Bill and Melinda Gates' scholarship pledge to minority students?
2. What kind of "backlash" occurred after actor Danny Glover complained about being passed up by New York cabdrivers, according to Jackson?

# I

America no longer has a race problem—or, at any rate, a racial *discrimination* problem. And if it does, the group most likely to be discriminated against is: white men.

I don't believe any of that, of course, and it's hard to see how any nonracist American can. But many do. As you might guess, I've been reading my mail again.

The anti-affirmative action mail no longer surprises. What does is the number of readers who weighed in to question Bill and Melinda Gates' billion-dollar scholarship pledge to bright minority youngsters. Surely there's no more conservative an idea than the right of rich people to do what they will with their own money. But listen:

"What would (your reaction) be if someone donated a billion dollars to be used for scholarships for needy white students? . . . Please explain why this situation is acceptable today and do so in such a way that I can feel thankful for the donation rather than resentful."

Or: "Is it true that a poor Caucasian from an economically distressed region need not apply for this scholarship? What percentage of 'minority' blood makes you eligible? I normally feel pretty middle of the road, but this strikes me as wrong and promoting the type of feeling that keeps races apart."

Or: "Had this gift been given only to whites, what article would you have written?"

## Being Nonwhite Is a Disadvantage

These writers, and dozens like them, thought the Gates Foundation's gesture was terrific—wished something like it had been available for them. What they resented was that eligibility for the benefit was based on race and ethnicity.

The respondents, it seems to me, acknowledge that poverty or geographical isolation are serious disadvantages but imply that race is not. Most black Americans—and many other minorities as well—would argue that being nonwhite is a special disadvantage all its own. Black folk get it when stand-up comic Chris Rock tells white people how they *really* view race: "Ain't one of you would change places with me," he says, "and I'm *rich!*"

His point (at the risk of overinterpreting a guy whose job

is to entertain) is that black people understand without having to think about it the advantage that comes from being white in America—that white people who "don't see race" are in fact blind to their own unearned and heritable advantage.

But Rock's zinger notwithstanding, many white people don't *feel* advantaged. Indeed, when it comes to matters like the Gateses' billion or affirmative action or various "diversity" programs, they feel disadvantaged. Just the other day, Gwen Ifill, the rapidly rising star of TV news, was telling a reporter how the networks had pursued her because of her obvious gifts, her record and that "bonus of bonuses, I'm a black woman."

There! Isn't that acknowledgment that her race is an advantage? Well, yes—but only in the context of a generalized racial disadvantage. For blacks, that context is so obvious as to be self-evident. If blackness were truly an overall advantage in television, would CNN (perhaps the most "diverse" of all the news networks) be the only one with a black anchor? Would African American and Hispanic civil rights organizations be complaining about the "white-out" or "brown-out" of the current network entertainment season? Would we even be talking about Ifill, the "first" nonwhite to moderate PBS's "Washington Week in Review"?

If Ifill enjoys racial advantage, it is rather like Colin Powell's racial advantage when he was being courted (by both parties) as a possible presidential candidate. Clearly his race made him more attractive—but in a context where being nonwhite is generally an all-but-insurmountable handicap.

## What Race Means

One thing more. The letters underscore two distinct views of what race means. For most blacks, white privilege, like black disadvantage, is an umbrella spread over a race. What other conclusion could you draw from the fact that all but a tiny handful of Fortune 500 CEOs are white, as are virtually all the heads of nonminority universities and 100 percent of the U.S. senators?

For my correspondents, those are stories of *individual* success. The fact that the holder of a particular post is, statistically, likely to be white doesn't mean that any particular white aspirant is likely to get it.

Can they really believe that all discrimination and disadvantage is individual, that *racial* discrimination is nothing more than a misleading abstraction?

Well, maybe they do.

# II

Even in an obvious injustice, apologists for racism find a way to say that all black men must pay for the sins of a few. African-American actor Danny Glover made a big stink about being passed up by taxicabs he tried to hail in New York City. Glover complained to the city's taxi commission after an episode in which five cabs sped past him, his college-age daughter Mandisa, and her roommate at New York University.

Mandisa Glover said: "It's embarrassing. There have been situations where I've had to ask" a white person "to hail a cab for me."

It is so embarrassing that even Mayor Rudolph Giuliani, hardly known for battling racism, announced an undercover crackdown on cabbies. "This is a good time to do it," Giuliani said. "It got a great deal of attention because it involved a person of great notoriety."

But not even Glover's box-office popularity could stop a backlash that tried to shift the blame from racism to black men. Several newspaper and television reporters and talk-show hosts made sure everyone knew that cabbies were mostly men of color. The media made sure these men gave the most colorful justifications why they pass up black men with quotes like "I don't want to take a chance to lose my life," and "Do we want to die?" In citing past black robberies and unpaid black fares, a black cabbie said, "You are supposed to stop for everybody, but do you really think cabdrivers are going to put our lives on the line? That is nonsense, and you can be sure 99 percent of the drivers agree."

## Paying the "Black Tax"

Helping to amplify the fear were conservative or confused columnists. One columnist, citing the fact that black men disproportionately commit crime, called it "prudence" for cabbies to pass up black men. Another quoted an African-American reporter for the *New York Times* who drove a cab when he was in college and passed up casually dressed black men. Another columnist wrote, "Keep it in perspective—some cabbies have been ripped off by blacks."

The clear implication is that African-Americans should shut up. We should soak and freeze patiently on street corners. We should cheerfully accept getting home an hour later than white folks after a rough day at work or midnight ordeals after a night on the town. We should willingly pay this black tax.

But many of the people who imply this take the opposite perspective when white people complain about being passed up. Take affirmative action. Even though white racism continues to perforate equal opportunity, America is deciding that no individual white person should be stranded on the corners of fairness.

Michael McLaughlin, who destroyed affirmative action at Boston Latin to make way for his daughter Julia and Sarah Wessmann, said: "The fact that blacks and Hispanics have a tougher time as a group is not something that can be put on the back of Sarah Wessmann." In killing affirmative action at the University of Texas Law School, white plaintiff David

Rogers said his purpose was to force the school to judge applicants "individually, not by the color of their skin." In pushing to eliminate affirmative action around the nation, Keven Nguyen, a spokesman for the American Civil Rights Coalition, said, "You shouldn't be treated differently because of the way you look."

White people, in this view, bear no burdens, past or present, from the wrongs of their brothers and sisters. The media obviously agree. Long practiced at tarring African-American families for their gang members, the media did not pathologize white culture or generalize about white families in the mass shootings and bombings by disaffected white males such as Timothy McVeigh, Jeffrey Dahmer, Kip Kinkel, Eric Harris, and Dylan Klebold. There is no generalizing allowed of white people, even though they are arrested—even in cities—for the majority of hate crimes and cases of drunken driving, forcible rape, aggravated assault, weapons possession, larceny, burglary, and drug abuse.

It is why presidents will go into the heart of black America to lecture and even embarrass black people on crime but never specifically address white people as white people to act as a community to end their violence and racism. In Oklahoma City and Columbine, violence and racism went hand in hand.

Low-income black people do disproportionately commit the majority of street robberies and murder. But law-abiding black people should not be stereotyped for that any more than white people should be looked upon as Klansmen because David Duke is white.

The forces that say that no individual white person should pay a price for institutionalized racism show their hand when they tell black folks to calm down about cabs. The "color-blind" America, where individuals bear nothing on their backs as they compete for school slots, jobs, and cabs, is reserved for white people. Black people are told to carry the weight of all black criminals on their back.

Even when black people fail to hail a cab, the meter in our souls is running. Affirmative action is being ended by people who say they "shouldn't be treated differently because of the way you look." Being told this and then watching the cabs go by is too high a fare to "keep it in perspective."

*"While teaching whites to hate themselves,
'diversity educators' are simultaneously
teaching 'people of color' to hate whites for
their racist oppression."*

# Political Correctness Leads to Reverse Discrimination

Part I: Paul Craig Roberts; Part II: Andrew Stephen

Liberal educational and social policies that advocate sensitivity about race and gender issues are often described as "politically correct." Many people believe that political correctness (PC) fosters reverse discrimination through the censorship of opinions considered to be offensive to minorities and women. The authors of the following two-part viewpoint maintain that PC limits free thought and victimizes people accused of allegedly racist or sexist behavior. In Part I, columnist Paul Craig Roberts argues that white college students encounter PC and reverse discrimination in "diversity education" programs that portray whites as evil and oppressive. In Part II, journalist Andrew Stephen contends that PC unjustly punishes people for rude behavior.

As you read, consider the following questions:

1. According to a Zogby poll cited by Roberts, what percentage of students believe that political correctness restricts their education and their speech?
2. What did Janice Barton do to receive a forty-five-day sentence for "insulting conduct in a public place," according to Stephen?

# I

Language was a prime factor in the murder of 6 million Jews by the National Socialists in Germany and 60 million to 80 million "class enemies" by Communists in Russia and China. Today, similar language is being used in American colleges and universities to annihilate the history, culture and self-esteem of white people.

Halls of learning have become reeducation camps, where legions of "diversity educators" and "sensitivity trainers" strive to "get inside" the minds of white students and replace private conscience, identity and belief with group guilt.

Propaganda and emotional manipulation are used to teach whites to think the best about "people of color" and the worst about themselves. Whites are cold, logical and distant ("ice people"). Blacks are warm, intuitive, empathetic and spontaneous. Whites are relentlessly acquisitive. Blacks are in harmony with nature. Whites as a group use the "power structure" that they control to victimize blacks as a group.

The most prominent of the reeducators is Jane Elliott. She teaches that "white people invented racism" and are a parasitic race who even stole the English language from people of color. She uses a film, *Blue Eyed*, to teach white students self-contempt and blood guilt for their racist evil.

Elliott thinks of herself as a kind, loving woman who is a tireless foe of racism. Corporations, government agencies and universities pay Elliott $6,000 a day to teach white people to hate themselves. The media lionize her. Disney plans to make a movie of her life.

## Universities as Reeducation Camps

While teaching whites to hate themselves, "diversity educators" are simultaneously teaching "people of color" to hate whites for their racist oppression. The "privilege" of white skin only can be remedied by legal privileges for blacks—thus, the necessity of racial quotas and affirmative action.

In the reeducation camps that masquerade as universities, it is an axiom that reverse discrimination is a myth. The discrimination that white students experience in university admissions and sensitivity training is not considered to be discrimination, but necessary reeducation to rescue whites from impermissible ways of being.

"Diversity educators" also deny that our culture is being Balkanized. What is really happening is that "evil racist white culture" is being stamped out, and whites are finding a new existence as allies of the oppressed. Once whiteness is extirpated, we all will be warm and intuitive and love one another.

---

## The PC Establishment

The New [Liberal] Establishment has replaced traditional mores and values with a relativistic "experimental society" that masquerades as "sensitive." Conservatives say it fails citizens of all races and genders and is spawning a new racism and sexism.

What started out as "tolerance" seems to many to have degenerated into lower standards, unfairness and discrimination. It has brought such programs as affirmative action, bilingualism, a mass hysteria of sexual harassment, "multiculturalism" instead of "uniculturalism," political correctness, weak college curriculum, irresponsible court decisions reaching up to the Supreme Court, a dubious coed military, distorted arts and an immigration policy that purposely penalizes Europeans—all within a framework of strict conformity in which fashionability reigns.

Martin L. Gross, *Insight*, October 27, 1997.

---

If you want to read more, consult Professor Alan Charles Kors' "Thought Reform 101" at www.reason.com or www.thefire.org. Kors, a brave man, reports that white students are experiencing the fate of Winston Smith, the fictional character in George Orwell's *1984*, whose "false consciousness" must be purged to make him fit with the new society. Kors says that the urge to "remold" whites has led reeducationists to pursue white students into "the ultimate refuges of self-consciousness, conscience and private beliefs" in an attempt to break down individual identity.

Such measures can foreshadow physical genocide. German intellectuals pursued the Jews with words for 60 years before the rise of Hitler. Lenin and his followers murdered "class enemies" first with words and then with reeducation camps. It is extraordinary that white taxpayers and donors are pouring billions of dollars into reeducation camps dedicated to the destruction of "white consciousness."

## Enforced Sensitivity Training

As happened under the Nazis and Communists, once a race or class is assigned collective guilt, all protections fall away. White students everywhere are experiencing the demise of due process and their First Amendment rights.

Christopher Monson is a student at St. Cloud State University in Minnesota, where he is an activist on behalf of increasing minority presence on campus. Recently, he argued that a public university had obligations to public access and that it would be illegal to prevent credit-card companies from soliciting on campus, just as "not allowing blacks on campus" would be illegal.

His harmless analogy was deemed "a racial insult." Monson was sentenced to sensitivity training by university president Suzanne Williams without a hearing or due process. This lawlessness at St. Cloud State is reminiscent of Nazi and Communist lawlessness. Once Jews were stigmatized, their rights as German citizens evaporated. The same happened to "class enemies."

The stigmatization of whites has reached the point where Williams did not blink an eye at exercising unconstitutional power over the free speech of Monson.

Students know the situation is out of hand. A recent Zogby poll found that 95.7 percent believe high academic standards and diversity of ideas are more important than ethnic diversity; 92.7 percent oppose racial quotas; 57.9 percent say there is too much politics in the classroom; and 55.4 percent say "political correctness" restricts what they can learn and say. Parents, donors and trustees need to find some courage before the Nazification of the universities is a fait accompli.

## II

In January 2001, a 14-year-old boy found himself facing the full might of the American judicial system. Shortly before Christmas, in what all concerned agree was teenage horseplay at a school in Espanola (population 11,276) in New Mexico, the boy slapped a 13-year-old girl classmate on her behind.

"The way I see it, they were just messing around," says the boy's grandmother. Even the girl's mother is rallying to the boy's defence: "I wouldn't have pressed charges, given that it was just a slap on the butt," she says. The girl herself insists that there was nothing sexual involved. "But why the buttocks?" was the retort of Espanola's police chief. "Why not the arm, why not some place else? It's the target area that concerns us." And so, as New Mexico's very own Inspector Starr sleuths his way into adolescent mating patterns, the boy faces not only the stigma of a conviction as a sex offender, but two years in a juvenile detention centre.

A couple of thousand miles north-east, meanwhile, the learned judges of the Massachusetts Supreme Court have been deliberating on a drawing made in school by an even younger boy. He had been sent out of class, and doodled a picture of his teacher begging for mercy as he pointed a gun at her. The doodling was confiscated, the drawing was deemed to constitute a threat to kill the teacher, and the boy was given five years' probation. In January 2001, lawyers argued that the drawing was protected under the freedom-of-expression First Amendment of the US Constitution: but that freedom "does not protect conduct that threatens another," the judges ruled. Schoolboy number two, not yet in his teens at the time of his crime, thus finds himself marked down as a dangerous criminal for life.

## The PC Conundrum

Welcome back, then, to the US phenomenon of political correctness. It may have spread worldwide since it took off as a concept following the 1987 publication of Allan Bloom's *The Closing of the American Mind*. But there is something uniquely American in the PC conundrum, whereby apparently good intentions coalesce to produce disastrous and sometimes downright fascistic results: In the year 2000, 45-year-old Janice Barton was leaving a restaurant in Michigan with her mother and daughter, when she overheard a couple speaking Spanish. "I wish these damned spics would learn to speak English," she said, not dreaming that one of them was actually a sheriff's deputy who also spoke English. The result: a 45-day sentence for "insulting conduct in a public place."

In all three instances, we can see initial good intentions: in New Mexico, that teenage girls should not have to put up with physical boorishness from boys; in Massachusetts, that the courts should protect teachers from potentially violent pupils; in Michigan, that racism is not on. All perfectly reasonable.

Yet, in all three cases, we also know that the authorities have gone too far; that officialdom has weighed down with monumentally inappropriate oppression on to two misbehaving boys and a silly middle-aged woman, ruining their lives and creating three more martyrs for foreigners who like a chuckle over those silly Yanks. Sadder still is that such cases provide fodder for the American right to shake its collective head over the effects of what are supposedly progressive forces.

## Political Correctness Undermines Liberal Ideals

The result is that progressive ideals quickly evaporate in the mix of political correctness. Puritanical witch-hunters, ever vigilant for latter-day baddies under the bed, alight on their prey with the zeal Americans have always used to hunt down suspected un-Americans of the era—be they, these days, schoolboys or middle-aged women. In theory, the socially progressive win; in practice, they merely hand propaganda weapons to their reactionary counterparts.

The tragedy is that when the Inspector Starrs of the PC police zoom into action, they are forsaking what should be the real targets: poverty and the vicious racism that still poisons the American bloodstream, whatever the superficial gloss of politically correct laws may seem to suggest. In their pyrrhic victory in introducing PC laws and policies, therefore, the supposedly progressive frequently set back their cause by generations.

I say "supposedly," because my sneaking belief is that those who pursue PC laws and rules most avidly are, subconsciously, often not seeking justice and fairness at all; they are usually from the complacent middle classes, comfortable with the status quo and merely seeking gratification that they are conforming to notions of equality and fairness for all. The wheel thus turns full circle, with the truly oppressed remaining oppressed while the consciences of those who could do something about it are appeased.

*"What some deride as 'political correctness'*
*is really only a caricatured description of*
*what I always defined as common decency."*

# Political Correctness Does Not Lead to Reverse Discrimination

Rebecca T. Alpert

Calls to limit behavior or speech considered to be offensive to minorities are controversial because many people believe such efforts have grown into a movement—"political correctness" (PC)—that suppresses free thought and open dialogue. In the following viewpoint, Rebecca T. Alpert maintains that so-called political correctness is usually an attempt to be genuinely sympathetic to and respectful of minority cultures and points of view. While critics of PC would encourage people to "be honest" and openly express their bigoted and hurtful opinions, Alpert believes that people should take on the challenge of learning why such opinions are misguided and offensive. Alpert, a Reconstructionist rabbi, is codirector of the Women's Studies Program at Temple University in Philadelphia, Pennsylvania.

As you read, consider the following questions:
1. In Alpert's opinion, when is honesty not a virtue?
2. Why was the author concerned about a classroom discussion spurred by a student's anti-Semitic comment?
3. What might account for the notion that African Americans are bad tippers, according to Alpert?

From "Coming Out of the Closet as Politically Correct," by Rebecca T. Alpert, *Tikkun*, March/April 1996. Copyright © 1996 by The Institute for Labor and Mental Health. Reprinted with permission.

Well, I admit it. I spend a fair amount of time and effort trying my best to be politically correct. I have never, for example, during a polite conversation, asked a heterosexual to explain to me about her activities in the bedroom, although they might seem exotic to me. And it's been years since I've told a joke that begins, "a priest, a rabbi, and a minister. . . ."

I have come under a fair amount of criticism for this behavior, and become the butt of many jokes in society these days. But I can't for the life of me figure out why, since I believe that what some deride as "political correctness" is really only a caricatured description of what I always defined as common decency; a variation on the Levitical precept that what is hateful to you, you should not do to others.

But these days, common decency seems to be out of style, replaced by the passionate desire to tell the truth, the whole truth, and nothing but the truth, no matter what the consequences to the listener. Like they do on those T.V. talk shows. And sometimes the results are tragic, as when a heterosexual man who learned on air on "The Jenny Jones Show" that he was the object of a gay man's affections shot his admirer.

## Free Speech Should Be Thoughtful

From my perspective, this kind of "let it all hang out and damn the consequences" type of honesty is not a good thing. First, inflicting pain is wrong. We Jews do not value suffering. When someone tells me that what I've said about them is hurtful, my impulse is to stop saying it. Nor do I really want to know all the lurid and evil thoughts that lurk in the minds of those who don't respect me.

Second, there is no great value to saying everything you think. Free speech is a complex ideal. It should be thoughtful and bold, not hateful and undisciplined. And honesty is not a virtue when it causes pain. My mother taught me about the moral value of occasionally telling small lies. (We used to call them "white lies.") Being PC, I don't use the phrase anymore, since it must be tiring for people of color to have white stand perpetually for all that is good. Besides, the English language is versatile; finding linguistic substitutes is half the fun of being politically correct. Not telling every-thing all the time, when your goal is to avoid hurting an-other person, is in fact a virtue. Learning when and when not to speak and what and what not to say is a value in itself.

You might conclude from my position on the virtues of si-lence that we were better off when gay men and lesbians never discussed our sexuality. Why do we get to be honest and our critics do not? Yet I do not accept this conclusion; it would be like suggesting that American Jews return to a time when assimilation was a primary value in our community, when we hid being Jewish. Honesty is appropriate when people talk about their own lives. Honesty is not appreciated when its goal is to suppress or trivialize a group to which you do not belong. Argue with me about what I think, but don't call me names or question my right to talk about my group's culture in public while you're doing it.

## Hurtful Words in a College Classroom

I came out as a lesbian in the progressive Jewish community when being PC was fashionable. And I came all the way out, as publicly as possible. I am politically involved in the gay, lesbian, bisexual, and transgendered community; my name and face are often in the news, and I write and teach on les-bian subjects in the Jewish world as well. It's a great strategy to avoid being wounded by others. I've never had my feel-ings hurt. I do not have to endure the silly questions and nasty remarks; no one would make them to my face, afraid of being politically incorrect. It's delightful to know that many people are afraid to say things that might offend me.

But when I came out as a lesbian, I also left the cocoon of progressive Jewish life. Inadvertently, I came out as a Jew in a less politically correct environment, a college campus. Contrary to right-wing rhetoric, students really do say what-ever they think. Now when I teach women's studies classes, I do not come out as a lesbian; it is too dangerous. But I do come out as a Jew, and in this environment, I find out what young people are thinking. And what they are thinking, and saying, is mighty frightening.

One day, when teaching about the imperative within tra-ditional Jewish life of charitable giving, or tzedakah, a student raised her hand and posed the following question: "How can you say that Jews give money as a religious precept? We all know how stingy Jews are." Now you might say that it was good that she said that; otherwise, how could I have had the opportunity to teach her to think differently? There is a point to that argument, to be sure. If we don't hear others' hateful and stereotypic notions, how can we combat them?

But I wonder if it was worth the price. Because her words were out there for others to hear, along with my words to combat them. And while several students challenged her anti-Semitism in the discussion, others spilled more poison into the conversation. Which words changed whose minds? I'm not sure. I do know that teaching that class had a profound effect on me, and the hurtful memories stayed with me. I wonder if this student even remembers the exchange.

## Learning to Sympathize with Others

Lest I appear totally righteous and capture only your pity for those of us who find ourselves victimized by those who mock political correctness, let me tell you about what happens to me when I'm in the position of having my own foot in my mouth; of not living up to my own standards of decency. I hope my strategies will prove instructive and useful.

Before I came out as a lesbian, I was indeed homophobic. That is to say, I experienced a sense of loathing at particular behaviors of my lesbian friends. These behaviors were not sexual ones; for many years before coming out I had erotic interests and sexual relations with girls and women. But the idea of a lesbian wedding, or lesbian friends having a baby, or even using the word "lesbian" to describe an identity made me very uncomfortable. In this case, my solution to my dilemma was to try it myself, and I must tell you it worked quite well.

While this suggestion may amuse you, let me remind you that Orthodox Jews suggest it frequently for their way of life. Just keep kosher for a few weeks, they say, and you'll see what joy it provides. I've tried that, too, by the way, with less success. But I believe the effort was crucial to my ability to sympathize with Jews whose existential choices differ from mine. Experimentation is important in our lives, if only to define better who we are and how we want to live. You never do know if you haven't tried. I am a great believer in the rabbinic injunction not to judge others until you've stood in their place. It helps temper one's righteousness a great deal, along with expanding one's horizons.

## The PC Label

"Political correctness" permeates our culture like no other soundbite of recent times. Although the debate in the universities has subsided somewhat, the phrase *politically correct* regularly appears on T-shirts and in newspaper headlines, TV shows, comic strips, and everyday conversations. The fear of being PC often reaches ridiculous proportions. In 1994, the Wilmette, Illinois, village board decided not to put a drawing of four children of different races on its village vehicle sticker because "it would take 'political correctness' too far" and would be "forcing people to promote diversity" in that nearly all-white suburb of Chicago.

"Political correctness" is a label slapped on an enormous range of liberal views—from environmentalism to multiculturalism to abortion rights. According to one writer, "It is P.C. to be in favor of affirmative action" and to "profess a belief in environmentalism, Palestinian self-determination, third world revolutionaries, and legalized abortion." By this definition, 90 percent of America is politically correct.

John K. Wilson, *The Myth of Political Correctness*, 1995.

This strategy is not always possible or appropriate. I should not take on African-American cultural behavior in order to deal with my racism, for example. But that doesn't mean I can't learn as much as I can about other communities. While I can't stand in their place, it is important to me to listen to their perceptions about what their place feels and looks like and to respect their desires to name themselves.

That does not mean asking them to teach me. It was from African-American women that I learned that it is not up to them to educate white people. And, of course, I know that myself. While I may teach Judaism in a classroom or provide conversion lessons for those who are interested, I get really tired of answering questions like, "What is Reconstructionism?", when I sense that the people who are asking me have no real commitment to understanding beyond this conversational sound bite. I'd much prefer that they read the book on Reconstructionism I wrote, which requires that they spend some time thinking about the subject. Now I just recommend it to people when they ask. And reading really is a good way to learn about other cultures. It opens up new awareness and allows you to see the multiplicity of a culture, rather than making one person be its representative for you. When you know something, or even a lot, about someone's culture and identity, it makes it easier to get to know them. And even to ask questions or say things that, if you are politically correct, you are at first afraid to ask.

## Different Cultures Deserve Respect

So having done all that sort of work—reading, observing, living in a multicultural environment—I think I know a lot now about African-American culture. Enough to teach a race and gender course, for example. While I know I don't know everything, I know how to find out. Another rabbinic saying suggests we learn most from our students, and this semester that was the case. One of the class assignments was to write about their daily experiences, noticing the way race and gender work in their lives. At this working-class university, several students wait tables for a living. Several of the white students shared the same anecdote about Black customers leaving bad tips. Now how was I going to counter that stereotype? I never even heard it before. And being the PC type that I am, I just assumed it was slanderous. They probably say that about Jews too, after all.

During this time I was reading Bebe Moore Campbell's novel, *Brothers and Sisters*. The protagonist, Esther Jackson, is an African-American woman banker. Out to lunch one day with her white colleague, Mallory Post, Jackson notices that the waiter hands the bill to Mallory and talks only to her. What kind of tip would I leave if I had been ignored like that? So, screwing up my courage and with my newfound knowledge, I asked an African-American friend about this. She said, yeah, many Blacks are lousy tippers. Some of it is the service, but some of it is a cultural thing. They see tipping not as something matter-of-fact, but as something that you earn with very good service (something blacks rarely receive).

The point of all this is that things that seem simple or exotic or alien or nasty about other cultures often are not. They are only different, can be explained logically, and deserve respect. So for me cultural relativism is O.K., but ethical relativism is not. I believe that people should not hurt others' feelings, and if they do they should take responsibility to educate themselves about why what they said was hurtful, admit their mistakes, and yes, apologize. And the people who were hurt might find it easier to forgive.

> *"Allowing blacks to be more racist than whites is in itself racist because it robs individual blacks of the expectation that they can be as moral as anyone else."*

# Minorities Should Take Responsibility for Reverse Discrimination

Andrew Sullivan

In the following viewpoint, Andrew Sullivan contends that blacks and other minorities who express prejudice against whites are rarely condemned for being racist. He points out that while white bigotry is strongly denounced, minority bias against whites—reverse discrimination—is tolerated by liberals who maintain that racism is a societal problem and not a personal moral choice. Sullivan believes that this liberal attitude is cowardly and reflects a racist double standard. In his opinion, no one—neither white nor minority—deserves any justification for berating people on the basis of race. Sullivan is a senior editor of the weekly magazine the *New Republic*.

As you read, consider the following questions:

1. According to Sullivan, what were Natalie Hopkinson's reasons for buying an expensive home in Washington, D.C.?
2. What argument about racism did liberals once hold sacred, in the author's opinion?
3. In Sullivan's view, what is the "fault line" in America's current cultural politics?

An almost remarkable piece ran in the June 24, 2001, *Washington Post*. I say "almost" because the *Post* has run articles before that reflect mild black hostility to whites. But it is still rare for even the *Post* or the *New York Times* to run articles that openly defend racial separatism as a goal in itself.

The article, by *Post* staffer Natalie Hopkinson, is a tale of how she and her husband moved to D.C. and bought an expensive Victorian house in the District's Bloomingdale section. Her intent was not merely to live in the District but to prevent white people from buying the house. In her words, "[T]he fact that we had emerged victorious from a six-month battle at the height of the District real estate wars—skirmishes in which we were often the lone black faces vying for homes in historically black neighborhoods—said something else: 'We damn sure are not about to let white folks buy up all the property in D.C.'"

Racial hostility to non-blacks pervades the entire piece. Hopkinson and her husband grew up in largely white middle-class neighborhoods and loathed the experience. They were, she says, subjected to bigotry. Her response is to return to a predominantly black city and keep it as segregated as she can: "There is a real sense among black Washingtonians that the city is slipping away from us. A few months ago, as I left a take-out on Georgia Avenue, a gentleman passed me a flyer. It invited me to a community meeting where residents planned to debate the question, 'Is the Chocolate City turning Vanilla?' I pocketed the flyer, but didn't bother going to the meeting. I already knew the answer: Not if I have anything to say about it."

## Racial Bitterness

In some ways, Hopkinson's commitment to return to the inner city—in contrast to the countless members of the black (and white) middle-class who have abandoned it—is admirable. She also sees no reason why white residents cannot also do their part: "Many whites want to help out, too, and their privileged racial status can only improve the city's prospects. But this is the Chocolate City. It's our responsibility as black people to return to these historically black communities that are finally rebounding." Notice that the whites do not bring their commitment, talent, or under-standing. Their only asset is their "privileged racial status."

This is not another battle about gentrification. Hopkin-son is not a longtime, poor black resident being squeezed out by higher rents. She's an affluent member of the black middle class and, like many bourgeois blacks, seems to view her success as reason to be more racially bitter, not less. She is a newcomer to a city she defines as her own solely because of the color of her skin. In her eyes, white residents of the Chocolate City, even if they have lived here all their lives, are not as authentic as she.

---

## On Racial Pride

I suspect . . . that when most black people embrace the term "racial pride," they mean more than that they are unembar-rassed by their race. They mean, echoing Marcus Garvey, that "to be [black] is no disgrace, but an honor." Thus when James Brown sings "Say It Loud—I'm Black and I'm Proud," he is heard by many blacks as expressing not just the absence of shame but delight and assertiveness in valuing a racial des-ignation that has long been stigmatized in America.

There is an important virtue in this assertion of the value of black life. It combats something still eminently in need of challenge: the assumption that because of their race black people are stupid, ugly, and low, and that because of their race white people are smart, beautiful, and righteous. But within some of the forms that this assertiveness has taken are important vices—including the belief that because of racial kinship blacks ought to value blacks more highly than others.

Randall Kennedy, *Atlantic Monthly*, May 1997.

---

Is this racism? The *Post* doesn't think so. But would the *Post* ever publish a piece by a white man who wanted to move back to, say, Cincinnati because it was once a predominantly white city, and who believed he had more right to be there than black newcomers and residents? Of course not. Just imagine the statement "There is a real sense among white Washingtonians that the city is slipping away from us" ap-pearing in the *Post*. Maybe in a Ku Klux Klan newsletter.

But the distinctions between right-wing racists and left-wing racists are increasingly hard to discern. The left now argues that, since racism is not a personal moral choice but a structural oppression, blacks de facto cannot be racists. Liberals now argue that, although some element of choice is involved in a racist statement or act, minorities—especially those who have suffered in the past—should have more leeway than whites in being bigots. Fewer and fewer members of the American intelligentsia still believe what liberals once held sacred—that there is never any excuse for shunning or condemning anyone because of his or her race. Hardly anybody still maintains that allowing blacks to be more racist than whites is in itself racist because it robs individual blacks of the expectation that they can be as moral as anyone else.

But Hopkinson's case is interesting because it presents the issue in extreme form. She is wealthy; she grew up in integrated neighborhoods; she has a stellar education; she is a newcomer to the city; and yet she still claims racial privilege in D.C. over whites, Latinos, Asians, and any others with the nerve to live and work in a city that desperately needs all the influx it can get.

You could argue, I suppose, that protecting a neighborhood's culture is not the same thing as racism. Hopkinson, however, is new to her neighborhood. She's not defending something that is already hers. She is staking a claim—on purely racial grounds—to a culture she has decided to embrace. In some ways, this is human. You can see why some Hasidic neighborhoods want to keep out gentiles to protect their culture; you can see why some gay neighborhoods fret about becoming straight yuppie paradises (once all the town houses have been fixed up). But the line between a legitimate desire to defend a way of life and an ugly aversion to living among people who are different is a crucial one.

It should be possible, for example, to retain the character of a predominantly black neighborhood while incorporating increasing numbers of whites, Latinos, and Asians. What's to stop newcomers from getting to know local manners, food, and neighborhood events, regardless of their ethnicity? One of the joys of my mixed neighborhood in D.C., for example, is the local Catholic church, St. Augustine's. Predominantly black, its liturgy is a unique blend of African American spirituality, Catholic ritual, and Gospel music. I may be a white

95

gay Catholic, but no one bats an eyelid if I show up in the pews. Why shouldn't, equally, my black neighbors appreciate the Korean food my local convenience store offers? Why shouldn't my straight friends have a beer every now and again at a gay bar? My local park, named after Malcolm X, hosts Salvadoran soccer games on weekday evenings. This is not, of course, what Malcolm X had in mind, but it's certainly close to the vision of Martin Luther King Jr.

## The Fault Line in Current Cultural Politics

Does this threaten the identity of the Chocolate City? Only if you identify a city on purely racial grounds. Resisting an attempt to wipe out or smother an entire culture is not the same as resisting people purely because of their superficial differences. That's why parochial Hasidim who shun outsiders are indeed offensive to liberal values. Ditto for white-ethnic neighborhoods where black people are subtly and not-so-subtly kept out. And ditto for black neighborhoods that make white interlopers feel unwelcome not because the newcomers are wealthy or racist but simply because they are white. The freedom of association to keep to one's own should be legal, as long as the government doesn't enforce it. But in a liberal culture, such separatism should be seen for what it is: an assertion that what we have in common as citizens and as human beings is less important than what separates us as members of racial, ethnic, or other groups. This, in many ways, is still the fault line in our current cultural politics. It hasn't gone away. In fact, the separatists' arguments are gaining force all the time—abetted by white liberals who should know better and who are too cowardly and guilt-ridden to take this evil on.

*"Most [whites] would rather bypass . . . the pain and suffering that is required when confronting one's complicity in . . . racism, and other forms of domination."*

# Whites Should Take Responsibility for White Privilege

Leny Mendoza Strobel

In the following viewpoint, multicultural studies professor Leny Mendoza Strobel argues that many whites fail to understand the complexities of racism because they are unable or unwilling to see the advantages that whiteness grants them. It is more comfortable, Strobel maintains, for whites to minimize the significance of racial and cultural differences than to recognize how society favors those with white skin. She concludes that whites need to learn more about the experiences of people of color and more honestly examine what it means to be white in the United States.

As you read, consider the following questions:

1. What are some of the "clichés" that Strobel has heard from her students when discussing racial issues in the classroom?
2. In the author's opinion, what type of thinking allows whites to avoid examining how whiteness privileges them?
3. In what ways do whites distance themselves from seeing their own unwitting participation in institutional racism, according to Strobel?

Excerpted from "Surrounding Ourselves with Difference," by Leny Mendoza Strobel, *The Other Side*, January 2000. Copyright © 2000 by *The Other Side*. Reprinted with permission.

Too often we assume racial issues are really about how people of color cope and survive in a society defined by White norms. But we will never find healing unless we are willing to ask: What does it mean to be White?

I tell my students that I am trying to work my way out of my job. I keep wishing for the day when I no longer have to teach about race relations or the politics of identity and difference. But the possibility still seems remote.

I teach multicultural studies in a small public university where all students must fulfill the ethnic studies requirement to graduate. In a typical classroom of forty students, only two or three are people of color; the rest are White, mostly from suburban, middle-class backgrounds.

Over the last five years, I have compiled a list of clichés that students invoke when discussing issues of race, class, ethnicity, gender, or sexual orientation. These clichés are not just evasions; some are heartfelt expressions of the students' opinions. They usually surface when students are feeling defensive, unwilling to be challenged, or just tired of these subjects.

I hear statements like: "That's just human nature. There'll always be an oppressor and an oppressed." "Why must we always emphasize our differences? We should emphasize our similarities." "I'm tired of White bashing. I don't have anything to do with what my ancestors did." "I'm not racist; my best friend is Black (or Latino, or Asian)." "There's nothing I can do about the past, so why should I feel guilty?" "You can't understand, you're not Black (Latino, Asian)." "Why can't we all just get along?" And the ever-popular "Whatever."

## Overly Simplistic Solutions

Unexamined, these clichés point toward overly simplistic solutions for healing our racial divide. Often, my students suggest that if we would just learn to treat each other as human beings, or as children of God, or as individuals with absolute freedom of choice, then we wouldn't have a problem—and we wouldn't have to talk about race. Most of them would rather bypass the difficulty—and yes, even the pain and suffering—that is required when confronting one's complicity in the projects of imperialism, colonialism, racism, and other forms of domination within U.S. society.

I find that many White students assume that issues of race and ethnicity are really about how people of color cope and survive in mainstream society. They often point to the success stories of "model minorities" as proof that if individuals just pull themselves up by the bootstraps, the system rewards them. Consequently, when people of color fail, it is perceived as personal failure.

The students who benefit most from these courses are those willing to struggle with the idea that Whiteness (White privilege, White supremacy) is the other side of the race issue. But this requires a complex understanding of how social structures support ideological premises—and that's a difficult hurdle for most students. The idea that they, the White students, might be implicated in this problem is a shocking revelation to most.

## What Does It Mean to Be White?

As a dramatic example of the impact of Whiteness, I show my students a video-documentary, *The Color of Fear*. In it a Black man, Victor, tells a White man, David, that there can be no dialogue on racism "unless you're willing to be changed by my experience, as much as I'm changed every day by yours." This opens a dialogue on race and its intertwined relationship with class, gender, language, and nationality.

For many White students, the relevant question the film raises is: What does it mean to be White? They start to see that they have often viewed Whiteness through an assimilationist paradigm, in which Whiteness is an unmarked category against which all other categories are measured. As Victor explains: "White has been made synonymous with being human."

He adds that people of color are dying from trying to be human by becoming White. And they're not alone. "You're dying it from it too," he tells David, the White man, "but you don't necessarily know it."

Equating being human with being White allows many in the dominant culture to avoid examining the ways Whiteness privileges them. They resist looking at their personal history, religion, and assimilation of "American values," their political and economic ideologies, and their attitude toward "difference."

Most of the White students I teach have been socialized and educated to think of themselves as autonomous human beings with the opportunity to pursue the "American Dream." So it doesn't occur to them that people of color might not feel the same way or experience their life in the same way. Yet persons of color, who live most of their lives in the shadow of racism, are the ones expected to disprove the stereotypes that accompany race.

## Understanding White Privilege

There is a growing body of literature and analysis that can help white people see that whiteness, though made to appear invisible to whites, is in fact a dynamic force that is used daily to oppress those who are not white and to privilege those of us who are. This invisibility is in large part what locks racism in place. As long as we do not have to see and acknowledge that we are given benefits and privileges simply because we are members of the dominant group, we can name racism as "black people's problem" or "Native Americans' problem" or the problem of some "Other." And as long as we can each assume an identity as an individual rather than as a member of the white race, we do not have to take any responsibility for racism.

Marian Groot and Paul Marcus, *Poverty and Race*, March/April 1998.

These White students also sincerely believe that our democratic society works the same for everyone. And because deep-seated cultural conditioning has disconnected them from the past, they become defensive when asked to deal with what that past has produced. Though this disconnection is slowly coming to consciousness and beckoning to be healed, too often students respond by seeking to avoid blame—and its accompanying guilt and shame. But in those instances when confronting the past leads to a sincere effort to understand how a nation's history of "other-ing" produces social and political differences that privilege one group over another, healing can and does occur. . . .

White students in my ethnic studies courses may come to realize that the ethnic experience is different from theirs, but there is a distancing that happens in their psyche. They may blame the problems on the U.S. cultural values of materialism or capitalism, or on government economic and foreign policies, but they stop short of looking at their lives and how they buy into the very values they're critical of. They even name patriarchy or White elite capitalist men who run the most powerful corporations. But when invited to locate themselves within this society's structures, there is discomfort. After all, they say, they are mere individuals who do not possess the power needed to transform these institutions.

Those who do look at their lives might begin a painful soul-searching by interrogating their grandparents' and parents' racial attitudes and perceptions, and how these get passed on to the next generation. It is not uncommon for a female student to say: "My parents are not racist; but I know that if I bring home a non-White boyfriend, they will be disappointed." Then a litany of rationalizations follow. (Often, those who do break these unspoken family rules do so out of rebellion. Frankerberg, author of *White Woman, Race Matters* states that even this behavior implies a commoditization of ethnicity, to use the "other" as an object for one's motives.)

## Entering the Dialogue

Recently, one of my students, Jill, asked me about a novel by Filipino-American author Jessica Hagedorn. The book, *Gangster of Love*, is about the way the lives of Filipino-Americans are shaped by the intertwined history of the United States and the Philippines. Jill's boyfriend is Filipino-American, and she thought the book would give her insight into his culture.

Jill was especially interested in folkloric creatures, the aswangs, and the tikbalangs (equivalent of vampires and sorcerers), mentioned briefly in the book. When I asked why, she admitted that she was fascinated by their exotic nature, their "otherness." Asked if she knew about the relationship between the United States and the Philippines—especially that the two countries had been at war and that the United States had colonized the Philippines until 1946—she admitted she did not.

I told Jill that to read this book is to ask herself: What do I, a White middle-class woman from the Midwest, have to learn from Hagedorn? What do I know about U.S.-Philippine relations? What do I know about Filipino-American lives? What do I—a fifth-generation American—know about the immigrant experience, about what "others" (non-White and non-European) must do to be assimilated into the U.S. culture? What does it mean to be American? Is being White and being American the same? How about being human and being American?

I suggested to Jill that asking these questions might reveal links between her personal history and that of Hagedorn's characters. Such a shared background would open up two possibilities. First, she could use it to critique the ideologies that shape U.S. hegemony and dictate the different paths for people's lives. She could ask where the breaks in the common human thread have occurred, how individuals are complicitous in creating and preserving them, and what she and others might do to re-attach the severed ends.

Second, the newly-discovered links between herself and the characters could open an inner dialogue that would uncover parts of herself as yet undiscovered. From this she could get to know herself better, love herself better, and love her Filipino-American boyfriend better.

Jill took up the challenge. She explored the questions, let herself be changed, relinquished her defenses, and entered the dialogue.

To help her on this journey, I gave Jill a quote from the Russian philosopher, Mikhail Bakhtin, who writes that we must surround ourselves with as much difference as possible. Bakhtin encourages us all to pay the most loving attention to those differences, because they might speak back to us and reveal to us who we are.

Bakhtin believes that we cannot really love ourselves just by looking in the mirror. We must let others tell us what they see in us; we must let them tell us who we are from their own locations. And out of this dialogue, we create Love. We create Art. Only then will it be possible to live together.

# Periodical Bibliography

The following articles have been selected to supplement the diverse views presented in this chapter.

Charles T. Canady — "Q: Should Washington End All Preferences in Hiring and Contracting? Yes: Discriminatory Preferential Treatment Undermines Fundamental American Ideals," *Insight*, April 27, 1998.

*Economist* — "In High Schools, Too: Reverse Discrimination," February 14, 1998.

Joseph E. Fallon — "The Europhobia of the U.S. Justice Department," *Social Contract*, Summer 1998.

Sue Fox — "Mi Casa No Es Su Casa," *Los Angeles Times*, November 21, 2001.

Marian Groot and Paul Marcus — "Digging Out of the White Trap," *Poverty & Race*, March/April 1998.

Margo Jefferson — "The Presence of Race in Politically Correct Ambiguity," *New York Times*, February 8, 1999.

John Leo — "When Rules Don't Count," *U.S. News & World Report*, August 7, 2000.

Herbert London — "Campus Orthodoxy a Serious Problem in U.S.: At Duke, Unpopular Letter to the Editor Provokes Death Threats Rather than Debate," *Bridge News*, May 21, 1999.

S.M. Miller — "My Meritocratic Rise," *Tikkun*, March 2001.

John O'Sullivan — "Preferences for (Almost) All: Affirmative Action Today," *National Review*, April 17, 2000.

Katha Pollitt — "I'm O.K., You're P.C.," *Nation*, January 26, 1998.

Paul Craig Roberts — "The Liberal Worldview Seeks to Crush Independence," *Insight*, August 21, 2000.

Andrew Stephen — "Still Haunted by the Ghosts of Slavery," *New Statesman (1996)*, December 4, 1998.

Robert Weissberg — "White Racism: The Seductive Lure of an Unproven Theory," *Weekly Standard*, March 24, 1997.

Frank H. Wu — "The Pragmatism of *Bakke*," *Black Issues in Higher Education*, June 25, 1998.

# CHAPTER 3

# Is Affirmative Action an Effective Remedy for Discrimination?

# Chapter Preface

The roots of affirmative action lie in the Civil Rights Act of 1964, which prohibited job discrimination based on age, race, religion, gender, or national origin. Initially affirmative action aimed to eliminate racial disparities in hiring policies; later the goals were extended to include college admissions and the awarding of government contracts. While equal opportunity laws ban discrimination, affirmative action policies go further by requiring employers and college admissions committees to take "affirmative" measures to achieve a balanced representation of workers or students. Such measures include aggressive recruitment techniques designed to enlarge the pool of qualified female and minority applicants as well as the use of race and gender as factors in hiring and admissions decisions.

Public support for affirmative action was strong in the late 1960s and early 1970s, when many Americans shared the civil rights goal of increasing opportunities for women and minorities. However, a backlash started to develop by the late 1970s, when critics began arguing that affirmative action led to preferences and special treatment for women and minorities. Race-conscious policies, in particular, began to provoke legal challenges from whites who contended that affirmative action was a form of "reverse discrimination." In the late 1970s court case *Regents of the University of California v. Bakke*, medical school applicant Allan Bakke claimed that the University of California denied him admission because he was white. Bakke's lawyers maintained that the school's practice of using quotas—retaining a certain number of slots for minorities—discriminated against qualified white applicants. The case went to the Supreme Court, which ruled that publicly funded schools may use race as a factor in admissions decisions but cannot set aside a fixed number of slots for minority students. Thus, the use of affirmative action quotas in hiring and college admissions was banned.

Additional challenges to affirmative action emerged in the 1990s. In 1992, four white students sued the University of Texas law school, claiming that they had been denied admission so that less-qualified blacks and Hispanics could attend the school. A regional appeals court overturned the affirmative action policy, ruling that the school could no longer elevate some races over others in its admissions decisions. In 1996, California voters approved an anti-affirmative action measure declaring that the state could not "discriminate against or grant preferential treatment to any individual or group on the basis of race, sex, color, ethnicity, or national origin in the operation of public employment, education, and contracting." In 1998, Washington voters approved a similar initiative calling for the end of state-sanctioned affirmative action programs.

Despite these recent rollbacks, affirmative action programs remain common, and not all challenges to race-conscious policies are successful. For example, in *Gratz v. Bollinger*, a case contesting race-based admissions policies at the University of Michigan, twenty Fortune 500 companies filed amicus briefs emphasizing the value of a diverse workforce. In December 2000, a federal judge ruled that the school's affirmative action program served a "compelling interest" by providing educational benefits derived from a diverse student body.

Clearly, the subject of affirmative action continues to generate differences of opinion among employers, voters, and policymakers. The following chapter explores various viewpoints on this controversial issue.

"*Affirmative action is still an important provider of opportunities to minorities and women.*"

# Affirmative Action Is Beneficial

Robert C. Scott

Since the 1960s, the U.S. government has advocated affirmative action to correct the effects of discrimination on women and minorities—typically by adopting strategies that increase female and minority representation in the workforce. In the following viewpoint, Robert C. Scott contends that affirmative action is still necessary to ensure equal opportunity for qualified minorities and women. Without affirmative action, Scott argues, women and minorities have a difficult time competing in a discriminatory job market that favors white males. Scott is a Democratic representative from Virginia.

As you read, consider the following questions:
1. How often do blacks and Latinos encounter discrimination when applying for jobs, according to Scott?
2. According to the author, what happened in California's universities after an antiaffirmative action measure went into effect?
3. What kind of racial and gender preferences do affirmative action critics ignore, in Scott's opinion?

Discrimination is still rampant in America. One needs to look no further than the thousands of studies, lawsuits and commission findings to conclude that discrimination remains a cold and damning reality. According to Department of Transportation testimony based on extensive study, when a black-owned construction firm and a white-owned construction firm with the same equity, credit and experience apply for a bond, the white-owned construction firm likely will receive 50 times more bonding than the identically situated black-owned firm. In addition to facing discrimination in bonding, it is well-documented that minorities and women are victims of discrimination when seeking access to capital and inclusion in the informal business social circles in which many important business decisions take place.

And discrimination in America is not limited to the area of bonding and contracting. In "testing studies," similar to police sting operations, identical candidates, with the exception of their race, are sent to apply for credit, rent a house or apply for a job. Guess what? Discrimination uncovered by these testing studies is far greater than even the most ardent supporters of affirmative action ever could have imagined in 1998.

A recent testing study conducted by the Fair Housing Council in the Washington area found that minorities are discriminated against 40 percent of the time they attempt to rent apartments or buy homes. A similar study conducted by employment testers of the Fair Employment Council and Urban Institute has revealed that African-American and Latino job applicants suffer blatant and easily identifiable discrimination once in every five times they apply for a job.

## The Most Effective Remedy

Of all of the responses to discrimination, the most effective in remedying it has been affirmative action. Affirmative action is still an important provider of opportunities to minorities and women. The careers of former Chairman of the Joint Chiefs of Staff Colin Powell, Secretary of State Madeleine Albright and even Supreme Court Justice Clarence Thomas all have been enhanced by affirmative action programs intended to ensure that well-qualified minorities and women have a fair chance to compete, despite the lingering effects of discrimination.

The Supreme Court's decision in *Adarand vs. Peña* reaffirmed the use of narrowly tailored race-conscious measures to remedy discrimination. This case, however, is being misrepresented to justify the repeal of remedial measures designed to end discriminatory practices. Justice Sandra Day O'Connor, writing for the majority in *Adarand*, states that "the unhappy persistence of both the practice and the lingering effects of racial discrimination against minority groups in this country is an unfortunate reality, and government is not disqualified from acting in response to it. When race-based action is necessary to further a compelling interest, such action is within constitutional constraints if it satisfies the 'narrow tailoring' test this court has set in previous cases." Any assertion that continuing affirmative-action programs is inconsistent with the court's holding in *Adarand* is completely without merit.

Government still has a moral obligation to remedy discrimination and programs which remedy discrimination are deserving of our support, not our condemnation. Even President Ronald Reagan once said, "Time and experience have shown that laws and edicts of nondiscrimination are not enough; justice demands that every citizen consciously adopt and accentuate a personal commitment to affirmative action."

Moreover, ending affirmative action would represent a unilateral surrender in our nation's continuing war against bigotry. Unfortunately, we know all too clearly how our world will look without affirmative action. Following the Supreme Court's 1989 decision which held that the minority-business program run by the city of Richmond, Va., was unconstitutional, cities were forced either completely to abandon or suspend temporarily their minority- and women-owned business programs while they were restructured to meet constitutional requirements. When minority- and women-owned contracting programs were eliminated, minority- and women-owned contracting dropped more than 95 percent. When Michigan eliminated its program, minority businesses were completely shut out of state construction contracting.

Although women and minorities comprise two-thirds of the national population, they only receive approximately 5 percent of the federal contracting dollars. And yet, the only

## The Necessity of Affirmative Action

Today, the persistence of a supermajority of white men in positions of power demands that we as a nation continue to pursue policies that enable women and people of color to compete fairly for these positions. While I am of the belief that those in power are very consciously holding on to it, some suggest that it is unconsciously held attitudes, rather than heavy-handed racist and sexist beliefs, that account for the disparities that persist. Whatever the case, it is clear that people in power continue to hire people like themselves as successors. Without affirmative action programs to impose consideration of a wider pool of applicants, we can hope for little change.

Jaime M. Grant, *NWSA Journal*, Fall 1998.

initiative we are considering repeals the one tool known to help provide the few opportunities women and minorities now receive.

California and Texas show us how resegregated our schools will be without affirmative action. In California, since prohibitions against affirmative action went in to effect, underrepresented minorities have been all but shut out of California's top schools. Although studies have shown that, once admitted, minority students perform just as well as their non-minority peers, not one of the 196 African-American student applicants was admitted to the medical school at the University of California, San Diego. At the University of California, Berkeley, and at the University of California at Los Angeles, law-school admissions for African-Americans fell more than 80 percent. At the University of Texas Law School, or UTLS, African-American admissions fell 88 percent and Latino admissions fell 64 percent. The drastic fall in Mexican-American admissions to UTLS is particularly alarming in light of a recent *New York Times* article stating that one in 11 Mexican-American lawyers in the entire country is a graduate of the University of Texas Law School.

Predictably, eliminating affirmative action in California and Texas has led to a heightened impact of the widespread and discriminatory white-male preferences that for generations have prevented minorities and women from enjoying full participation in these states. Without the counterbalancing effect of affirmative action, culturally biased tests and admission standards, such as legacy preferences, have contributed to the near extinction of minorities admitted to schools in California and Texas.

## The Importance of Equal Opportunity

When affirmative-action programs have been abandoned, minorities and women have had a very difficult time competing against the bonding and loan preferences granted to white males. Affirmative action minimized the effect of preferences which have placed minorities at a disadvantage. The opponents of affirmative action, however, have ignored those preferences and have labeled initiatives designed to end invidious discrimination as "preferences." A flexible goal is not a preference; it merely provides accountability. Without goals and timetables to show progress in ending discriminatory practices, there is no mechanism by which to measure changes in practices of those who have been found guilty of discrimination.

We cannot ignore the real-life experience of antiaffirmative-action legislation: When affirmative action programs are ended, opportunities for women and minorities plummet.

Are the opponents of affirmative action content that our universities are being resegregated? Are those who wickedly invoke the words of the Rev. Martin Luther King Jr. in their rhetorical attacks on affirmative action happy that on the 30th anniversary of King's assassination, Congress is considering a bill that would lead to the resegregation not just of California and Texas, but the entire country? Are we a stronger and more productive country when minorities and women, more than 66 percent of the population, are denied equal participation in our economy?

It is time that we join our business and military leaders in their struggles to make this country as competitive as possible by enlisting the participation of all Americans, instead of excluding the overwhelming majority consisting of minorities and women. Without affirmative action, we will turn the clock back on progress we have made during the second half of the 20th century. [At this time], we should be bringing people together and increasing opportunities for all Americans, not just a select few.

*"[Affirmative action] preferences don't stop discrimination. Preferences are discrimination."*

# Affirmative Action Is Counterproductive

Roger Clegg

Roger Clegg is vice president and general counsel of the Center for Equal Opportunity, a Washington, D.C.-based think tank. In the following viewpoint, Clegg argues that affirmative action has led to race- and sex-based discrimination in American institutions. "Minority-group status" should not be used as a factor in hiring or college admissions decisions, he maintains; to do so creates unfair preferences for women and nonwhites who may not be qualified for the positions they seek. The best way to achieve continued progress in civil rights is to enforce antidiscrimination laws fairly and stop the use of racial and gender preferences, asserts Clegg.

As you read, consider the following questions:
1. What is Clegg's response to the claim that "only 'qualified' applicants are given preferences"?
2. In the author's opinion, why are many minorities not prepared to compete for coveted positions?
3. What kind of diversity matters, in Clegg's view?

We have to start by defining terms. Conservatives don't oppose some kinds of affirmative action—like aggressive antidiscrimination measures, or broadening outreach and recruitment in race-neutral ways—but they do oppose the use of preferences based on race, ethnicity, or sex. Such discrimination was never a good idea, and it certainly isn't now.

While we do not have a color-blind society, we have made enormous progress in a very short period. The best way to ensure continued progress is to declare victory in the civil rights war, enforce our antidiscrimination laws evenhandedly, and get on with our national life.

The real problems faced by American society have nothing to do with discrimination, and the use of preferences makes race relations worse, not better. The obvious costs of preferences—their unfairness to workers, students, and small businesses, in particular; the precedent they set for "permissible" discrimination; the resentment and stigmatization they cause; the economic and human costs of mismatching people and positions—outweigh any conceivable benefits. And the more institutionalized the use of preferences becomes, the harder it will be to get rid of them.

## Myths About Preferences

The defenders of preferences are stubborn, but their arguments are few—I had to stretch to make 10—and weak. Here is what they argue and why they are wrong.

*1. A preference "is just one factor."* Either race, ethnicity, or sex influences a decision, or it doesn't. If it doesn't, then why consider it at all? If it does, then in those cases certain people are getting something (and someone else is not getting something) because of their melanin content, where their ancestors came from, or their gender. That's unfair.

Always put the shoe on the other foot. Imagine someone told you: "True, I prefer whites over nonwhites, but I use race as only one of many factors. I also consider the person's grades, test scores, economic background; that someone isn't white works against them only in really close cases." Everyone would agree that was still discrimination. If you use race (or sex) as a factor, even one of many factors, you're dis-

113

criminating. That's true regardless of which race or sex you're discriminating against.

In any event, race is often an overwhelming factor. According to Harvard Professor Stephan Thernstrom, for instance, "among the most selective and prestigious [law] schools, 7.5 times as many black students were admitted as would have been the case if academic qualifications alone had been taken into account." The Center for Equal Opportunity has documented similar discrepancies in undergraduate admissions.

2. *Only "qualified" applicants are given preferences.* The issue is not whether the winning applicant is in some absolute sense "qualified." If you use race (or sex) to select a less qualified applicant over a more qualified one, you're discriminating.

Again, put the shoe on the other foot. Imagine someone told you: "I'd never select an unqualified white over a qualified nonwhite. It's just that when there are two qualified applicants and the nonwhite is more qualified than the white, I might select the white despite that." Not very reassuring to a nonwhite, is it? The people who were admitted to law schools when they were segregated were all "qualified." But this was still discrimination. It was still unfair to those who were discriminated against.

Besides, it is not clear that preferences are given only to people who are even minimally qualified. There are, for instance, dramatic differences in the graduation rates between those belonging to groups who are given preferential treatment by a given university and those who are not, as well as dramatic differences in their respective rates of passing bar exams (for lawyers) and board certifications (for doctors).

## Race and Sex Discrimination Is Wrong

3. *We have preferences for children of alumni, so why not race preferences?* We didn't fight a civil war over alumni preferences.

Discriminating based on race and sex is different from discriminating based on other attributes, like athletic ability or parents' alumni status. That's why Title VII of the Civil Rights Act of 1964, for instance, bans race and sex discrimination but not discrimination based on height or wealth or alumni status or veteran status. That's why the Fourteenth

Amendment has been read to ban race and sex discrimination but not most other kinds of discrimination. If it is wrong to prohibit race and sex discrimination and not other forms of discrimination, then Title VII and the Fourteenth Amendment are equally wrong.

Maybe some of these other preferences are unfair, too, but that doesn't make preferences based on race any more acceptable. If you want to stop alumni preferences, fine. Use whatever admissions criteria you want—except race, ethnicity, and sex.

*4. Quotas are already illegal. Surreptitious* quotas still exist, even if they are hidden because of their illegality.

But the real point is that, even if rigid quotas are not used, preferences certainly are. And a preference is just as discriminatory as a quota.

*5. Racism still exists.* There will always be *some* racism. If we keep preferences until there is no discrimination, then we will always have preferences.

And preferences don't make race relations better. They make race relations worse.

Preferences don't stop discrimination. Preferences *are* discrimination. There are other ways to stop discrimination besides preferences.

## No Justification for Discrimination

*6. Studies show recipients of preferences have been successful.* The two studies generally cited for this proposition—one published by the *New York University Law Review* and one by the *Journal of the American Medical Association*—are deeply flawed. Professor Thernstrom carefully discusses how the former actually supports the opposite proposition and briefly explains why the latter is "junk social science" in the December 1997 issue of *Commentary* magazine. The former study has also been debunked by another law professor, Gail Heriot. The graduation rates for the supposed "beneficiaries" of preferences are in fact much lower than for other students.

In any event, the fact that some who benefit from discrimination become successful would not justify the discrimination. The victims of the discrimination would have been as or more successful.

*7. Standardized tests (e.g., the SAT) are inadequate measures.* No one suggests that the SAT be used by itself to select students, but the fact is that, especially when used in conjunction with high school grade point averages and other information, the SAT is a very valuable tool. For one thing, it's much less subject to inflation than grades and recommendations.

Besides, if someone objects to the way the SAT is being used, that is no excuse for using preferences *on top of* the SAT. If the use of the SAT is flawed, then it should be changed for everyone, not just for some groups.

Again, select students however you like—just don't consider race, ethnicity, or sex.

## A Threat to Equality

The debate about affirmative action preferences is fundamentally about the rights and responsibilities of American citizenship. It is about whether we will have a system of government and a social system in which we see each other as equals. Although often lost in the rhetorical clamor about its benefits, race-based affirmative action as a concept is, at its core, a challenge to the relationship between individuals and their government. It is a direct threat to the culture of equality that defines the character of the nation.

Ward Connerly, *Hoover Digest*, Winter 2001.

*8. Without preferences, many institutions would be lily white.* If preferences were abolished, in many cases it would help some minority groups and hurt others. For instance, a college with an increased number of Asian students is not "lily white."

Furthermore, the minorities who no longer get into one school because of its color-blind policies will still be able to get into other schools—where their qualifications and graduation rates will now be on par with the rest of the student body.

In any event, any drop-off in minority admissions rates will simply show (1) the extent to which preferences were being used and (2) the degree to which those minorities were disproportionately not prepared to compete, probably because of deteriorating family structure and public schools. Better to address those problems directly, rather than sweep them under the rug.

# What About Diversity?

*9. Diversity makes our institutions stronger.* Abolishing preferences does not mean that there will be no more diversity. For one thing, most institutions are not likely to experience a dramatic change in their makeup. And there is no reason why *every* institution must achieve perfect demographic balance.

Moreover, the diversity that matters is not diversity of external characteristics like skin color, ethnicity, or sex. Abolishing preferences based on those characteristics does not prohibit selection of people with different or unusual ideas or experiences.

Finally, even if there are some possible benefits to using preferences in some situations, this does not justify the overwhelming costs the widespread use of such preferences have had: the lost opportunities for the victims, the message that it is sometimes permissible to discriminate, the resentment among nonminorities, the stigmatization of minorities, the selection of less qualified people, the mismatching of people and positions.

*10. Preferences are needed to correct and prevent discrimination.* No, they're not. There are already many federal and state laws on the books making it illegal to discriminate against minorities and women. Moreover, although discrimination still exists, it is nowhere near the problem it was just a generation ago. Let's not deny that fact.

It makes no sense to "solve" the problem of young black males not being able to get taxicabs by giving preferences to medical school applicants who happen to share the same skin color. You don't solve discrimination in one area of society by creating new discrimination in a different area.

You can't undo the discrimination against some blacks by some whites in the past by requiring new discrimination on behalf of different blacks against different whites.

The solution to the discrimination that exists is not more discrimination. It is to enforce the laws we have and to stop discriminating.

*"It is fair and equitable to consider race
and ethnicity as one factor among many
. . . in admitting qualified youths to
highly competitive universities."*

# Affirmative Action in College Admissions Is Necessary

Chang-Lin Tien

Affirmative action in college admissions is a fair way to provide equal opportunity for minority students, contends
Chang-Lin Tien in the following viewpoint. Racial divisions
still exist in American society, and including race as a factor
in admissions decisions is one way to ensure that promising
minority students have access to higher education. Moreover, Tien argues, affirmative action programs benefit all
students because they foster diversity and racial tolerance on
college campuses. Because it promotes interaction between
people of different backgrounds, affirmative action can be an
effective tool in bridging racial divisions. Tien is a former
chancellor of the University of California in Berkeley.

As you read, consider the following questions:
1. How will America's diversity affect what students learn
   in U.S. colleges and universities, according to the
   author?
2. According to Tien, how did administrators at the
   University of California in Berkeley work to maintain
   diversity after the state ended public-sector affirmative
   action?

From "In Defense of Affirmative Action," by Chang-Lin Tien, *USA Today*,
November 1997. Copyright © 1997 by the Society for the Advancement of
Education. Reprinted with permission.

When the debate over affirmative action in higher education exploded, my open support surprised many. My personal view about using race, ethnicity, and sex among the factors in student admissions has put me at odds with many, including the majority of the Regents of the University of California who govern my campus.

With California voters having decided in November 1996 to end all state-sponsored affirmative action programs, silence would seem to be a far more prudent course for me to take. Educators already have enough battles to fight—declining public funding, controversy over the national research agenda, and eroding public support for America's academic mission.

Why did I take on the explosive issue of affirmative action? My participation in the debate is inspired both by my role in higher education and my experience as an immigrant of Chinese descent. As chancellor of the University of California, Berkeley, I had seen the promise of affirmative action come true. Today, no ethnic or racial group constitutes a majority among the university's 21,000 undergraduates. Berkeley students enter better prepared and graduate at the highest rate in our history. Through daily interaction in classrooms, laboratories, and residence halls, they develop a deep understanding of different cultures and outlooks.

As an immigrant, I know the U.S. is the land of opportunity. Unlike any other nation in history, America has taken pride in being built by immigrants and allows foreign-born people like me to participate in the world's greatest democracy.

In 1956, I came here for graduate studies, a virtually penniless immigrant from China with a limited grasp of the language and customs of the U.S. A teaching fellowship was my income. To stretch my frugal budget, I walked across town to eat at the least expensive restaurants and scouted out the lowest-cost washing machines and dryers.

As a result of the wonderful educational opportunities I have enjoyed, I have contributed to America. My research in heat transfer has enhanced our engineering expertise in many critical technologies, including nuclear reactor safety, space shuttle thermal design, and electronic systems cooling. My former students teach and conduct research in America's top universities and industries. I was privileged to head the university with the largest number and highest percentage of top-ranked doctoral programs in the nation.

## The Harsh Realities of Discrimination

Yet, along with opportunity, I have encountered the harsh realities of racial discrimination that are part of America's legacy. Like it or not, this history of racial division is linked with the debate over affirmative action. Although the U.S. has made great strides, race still divides our society. It is part of the debate over how we afford equal opportunities to everyone.

My first months in the U.S. reflect how opportunity and racial intolerance can be linked. I served as a teaching fellow for a professor who refused to pronounce my name and only referred to me as "Chinaman." One day, the professor directed me to adjust some valves in a large laboratory apparatus. When I climbed a ladder, I lost my balance and instinctively grabbed a nearby steam pipe. It was so hot, it produced a jolt of pain that nearly caused me to faint, but I did not scream out. I stuffed my throbbing hand into my coat pocket and waited until the class ended. Then I ran to the hospital emergency room, where I was treated for a burn that completely had singed the skin off my palm.

My response seems to fit the Asian model minority myth: Say nothing and go about your business. My silence had nothing to do with stoicism, though. I simply did not want to endure the humiliation of having the professor scold me in front of the class.

Today, after four decades of major civil rights advances, members of racial and ethnic minorities like me no longer are intimidated into silence. Still, serious racial divisions remain. Those of us who are of Asian, Latino, or Middle Eastern heritage have become accustomed to having passersby tell us, "Go back to your own country." More typical is the polite query: "What country do you come from?" It makes no difference if you are first-generation or fifth-generation. If you have Asian, Latino, or Middle Eastern features or surname, many Americans assume you were born in another country. The ancestors of a professor in the university's School of Optometry left China to work in California during the 1850s. Even though his roots run far deeper than those of the vast majority of Californians, people invariably ask him where he was born.

## Attacking the Problem

Our nation can not afford to ignore the racial strife that continues to divide America. Nor should we forget that the U.S. is a great democracy built by diverse peoples. It is critical to attack the problem of racial division and build on national strengths. The finest hope for meeting this challenge will be America's colleges and universities.

These institutions launched affirmative admissions programs to open their doors to promising minority students who lacked educational and social opportunities. Over time, the composition of America's college students has changed. Campuses are more diverse than at any time in history.

Critics of continuing race or ethnicity as a consideration in student admissions argue that affirmative action unfairly discriminates against white and Asian-American applicants who worked hard in high school and received top grades. They further maintain that it no longer is needed to provide opportunities. Although I agree that affirmative action is a temporary measure, the time has not yet come to eliminate it. Educational opportunities vary dramatically in U.S. public schools.

The inner-city student can find illegal drugs more readily than computer labs and after-school enrichment courses. In contrast, the more affluent suburban student is hooked into the Internet, enrolled in honor classes, and looking forward to summer instruction.

Given this reality, it is fair and equitable to consider race and ethnicity as one factor among many—including test scores and grade-point averages—in admitting qualified youths to highly competitive universities. Such an approach remains the most effective way to make sure America does not turn into a two-tiered society of permanent haves and have-nots.

Assisting promising students is not the only reason for preserving affirmative action. The diversity of students, faculty, and staff that it inspired is one of the most exciting and challenging phenomena in American higher education today. All students stand to gain, whether they are whites, Asian-Americans, or traditionally underrepresented minorities.

I believe students on campuses that lack diversity can gain just a limited, theoretical understanding of the challenges and opportunities in a highly diverse nation. A lecture on Toni Morrison's novels or the theater of Luis Valdez is not enough.

No career or profession will be untouched by the rapid socio-demographic change. For instance, consider how America's diversity will affect those in U.S. colleges and universities. Education students will teach many youngsters born in different countries. Medical students will treat many patients with beliefs and attitudes about medicine that differ from the Western outlook. Students of engineering and business will work for major corporations, where they will be expected to design, develop, and market products that sell not just in the U.S., but in markets around the world. Law students will represent clients whose experience with the judicial system in their neighborhoods and barrios is distinctive from the way middle America regards the law.

## A Matter of Diversity

Diversity in colleges and universities benefits all students, not just the underrepresented minorities. Our experience at Berkeley shows the promise of affirmative action. Every time I walk across campus, I am impressed by the vibrant spirit of our diverse community. Nowhere do you see this better than teeming Sproul Plaza, where dozens of student groups set up tables representing a wide range of social, political, ethnic, and religious interests.

At Berkeley, undergraduates are about 40% Asian-American; 31% non-Hispanic Caucasian; 14% Hispanic; six percent African-American; and one percent Native American, with the rest undeclared. About one-quarter of freshmen come from families earning $28,600 a year or less; another quarter from families that earn more than $90,000. The median family income reported for 1994 freshmen was $58,000.

Young people from barrios, comfortable suburbs, farm towns, and the inner city come together at Berkeley to live and study side by side. Not surprisingly, they find first-time interactions with students from different backgrounds occasionally fraught with misunderstanding and tension.

As chancellor, I made it a point to listen and talk with students. Casual conversations as I walked the campus to meetings, dropped in at the library after work, and sat in on classes gave me greater insight into the day-to-day lives of Berkeley students. They told me about the practical challenges of moving beyond the stereotypes and learning to respect differences.

---

## The Benefits of Diversity

Professor Alexander Astin surveyed 25,000 students in 217 four-year colleges, assessing attitudes, values, beliefs, career plans, achievement, and degree completion. He found that emphasis on diversity is associated with "widespread beneficial effects on a student's cognitive and affective development." "[T]he weight of the empirical evidence," he concluded, "shows that the actual effects on student development of emphasizing diversity and of student participation in diversity activities are overwhelmingly positive." Professor Astin's research also shows that students who interact more with students of different backgrounds tend to be more successful in college, and that students' direct experiences with diversity are positively associated with many measures of academic development and achievement.

Martin Michaelson, *National Forum: The Phi Kappa Phi Journal*, Winter 1999.

---

Some African-Americans and Latinos confided they sometimes believed their professors and white classmates considered them to be inferior academically. This made them feel isolated from the general campus community. Some whites told me they felt like they had been pushed out by less-deserving blacks and Latinos. They also believed that overachieving Asians were depriving them of educational opportunities.

The views of Asian-Americans differed. Some were disturbed by the "model minority" stereotype. They complained that it pits them against other minorities and masks the problem of discrimination they still face. Others were concerned about issues such as affirmative action. They believed it is fair to base admissions on academic qualifications alone—which would open the door to more Asian-Americans.

These differing outlooks are not cause for alarm. Instead, they reflect the views held in society at large. It is important that students of all racial and ethnic groups told me they valued the opportunities on our campus to come together with people of diverse backgrounds. I believe it is this attitude our campus must reinforce as we help them to address differences.

The residence halls are the first place students come together. Because we understand the challenges associated with living together with those who have different values and outlooks, we run programs that encourage students to discuss racial and cultural differences openly.

Our campus tradition of academic freedom is critical. When issues arise where students are divided by race, they don't ignore the matter. We encourage all members of the campus community to air differences freely in forums, seminars, and rallies. Whether the topic is affirmative action, . . . or the organization of ethnic studies, students and faculty passionately debate the pros and cons.

Let me cite an example. In 1995, the longstanding conflict between Israelis and Palestinians led to fiery exchanges between Jewish and Muslim students on our campus. During rallies and counter-protests, an Israeli flag was ripped apart, while Muslim students alleged they were being demonized.

We addressed the issues directly. The campus held meetings to denounce "hate speech," while open debate was encouraged. My top objective was to make sure that discussions on this charged issue did not degenerate into racial epithets. I decided to forego an invitation from Pres. Bill Clinton to attend a White House meeting so I could meet with students who were central to the debate and help them hammer out their differences.

It is this tradition of study and debate that makes American higher education so valuable. Colleges and universities are a haven for open discussion. Only by addressing differences directly can students reach a deeper understanding of the real meaning of diversity.

## A New Challenge

Today, our campus faces a major new challenge. The University of California Regents have voted to end the use of race, ethnicity, and sex as a factor among many others in student admissions at its nine campuses in 1998. At first, the Regents' decision stunned me. I questioned whether we could preserve the diversity which is so important to our campus after losing an important tool for achieving student enrollments that reflect California's wide-ranging population.

Yet, I quickly realized the importance of the Regents' reaffirmation of their commitment to diversity even though they discarded affirmative action. So, I decided to take the Chinese approach to challenge. In Chinese, the character for crisis actually is two characters: One stands for danger and the other for opportunity. For me, times of crisis present both challenges and opportunities.

The end of affirmative action at the University of California gave us the impetus for trying new approaches to improving the eligibility rates of high school students traditionally underrepresented in higher education. At Berkeley, we set to work right away to turn challenge into opportunity. We realized our efforts would be doomed unless we worked even more closely with the public schools. Within weeks of the affirmative action decision, I joined the superintendents of the San Francisco Bay Area's major urban school districts to announce our new campaign to diversity: The Berkeley Pledge.

The announcement made it clear that our campus would not shirk its commitment to diversity. Instead, we pledged to step up the drive to support the efforts of disadvantaged youth to qualify for admission and preserve access to higher education. I committed $1,000,000 from private gifts, and we are seeking additional private support to fund this innovative approach.

America has come a long way since the days of Jim Crow segregation. It would be a tragedy if our nation's colleges and universities slipped backward, denying access to talented, but disadvantaged, youth and eroding the diversity that helps to prepare the leaders of the 21st century.

I find one aspect of the debate over affirmative action to be especially disturbing. There seems to be an underlying assumption that if it is eliminated, the nation will have solved the problems associated with racial division. Nothing could be further from the truth. It is critical for America to

125

address the issue of how people from diverse backgrounds are going to study, work, and live in the same neighborhoods together in harmony, not strife.

This is the challenge in higher education. It demands the collaboration of students, faculty, staff, and alumni at universities and colleges across America. All must work together to maintain the diversity that is essential to excellence.

*"Affirmative action encourages minorities to think of their prospects as determined by their race, a view that has had a devastatingly subversive effect on the attitudes of many young blacks toward academic achievement."*

# Affirmative Action in College Admissions Is Harmful

Jason L. Riley

Many analysts have claimed that affirmative action in higher education promotes equal opportunity and diversity on campuses, which in turn provides a healthy educational environment that benefits all students. *Wall Street Journal* editorialist Jason L. Riley contests this view in the following viewpoint. For one thing, recent lawsuits have revealed that college admissions guidelines often discriminate by allowing less-qualified minority students to be selected at the expense of qualified whites. Furthermore, Riley asserts, there is no credible evidence that racial diversity enhances academic achievement. In fact, he concludes, using racial preferences to foster diversity may actually intensify racial divisions and stereotypes.

As you read, consider the following questions:

1. What was Justice Lewis Powell's opinion in the case of *Regents of the University of California v. Bakke*, according to the author?
2. In comparison to whites, how much higher is the drop-out rate for blacks admitted to elite schools under preferential quotas, according to Riley?

The 1990's were not especially kind to the supporters of affirmative action in higher education. Although neither Congress nor the two successive occupants of the White House saw fit to take a stand against the increased entrenchment of racial preferences in our universities, some states and courts did. In 1996, the voters of California gave their approval to Proposition 209, which prohibited the state from using race as a factor in, among other things, the admissions process of the vast University of California system. The state of Washington followed suit two years later, and in 1999 Florida put an end to race-based programs at the state's ten public universities.

A greater blow still was the 1996 decision by the U.S. Court of Appeals for the Fifth Circuit in the case of *Hopwood v. State of Texas*. Scrutinizing affirmative action in higher education more closely than the federal judiciary had done for decades, the court overturned the admissions procedures of the University of Texas law school, which had systematically applied lower standards to black and Hispanic candidates than to whites. According to the Fifth Circuit, such disparate treatment was a gross violation of the Fourteenth Amendment's guarantee of "equal protection of the laws"—a ruling whose logic, if embraced by the Supreme Court, would effectively call a halt to preferential quotas at public universities.

Not that *Hopwood* went unchallenged, or that its intent has been fully carried out even in the states under the Fifth Circuit's jurisdiction. Both there and in other places where the public or the judicial system has voiced its disapproval of quotas, procedures have been put in place to circumvent or otherwise mitigate the consequences. As a recent survey by the Center for Equal Opportunity shows, preferential quotas continue to "run high and deep throughout public education."

In most such schemes, however, the goal itself has been redefined. No longer do college administrators and other affirmative-action advocates speak, as they once did, about the need to overcome a legacy of past discrimination or to achieve social justice. In seeking to justify race-based admissions programs, they now speak, rather, of a purely educational purpose: namely, "diversity."

It was thus with an audible sigh of relief that the affirmative-action lobby received the news, in December 2000, of a court decision favorable to its cause. In a ruling clearly meant as a counterweight to *Hopwood*, and based on the grounds, precisely, of "diversity," a federal judge in Detroit found the University of Michigan's system of admitting white and minority applicants under different criteria to be constitutionally sound. If the far-reaching decision in the case of *Gratz v. Bollinger* is upheld (it is now on appeal), the day may never arrive when affirmative action—a program once considered temporary even by its most ardent proponents—will finally come to an end.

## The *Bakke* Case

The "diversity" rationale did not come from nowhere. As with much else in the controversy over affirmative action in higher education, the inevitable starting point is the Supreme Court's historic ruling in the 1978 case of *Regents of the University of California v. Bakke*.

In 1972, a white man named Allan Bakke had applied for admission to the medical school of the University of California at Davis and been rejected. A year later, he applied again and was once more denied admission. Upon learning that sixteen of the 100 places in the class had been reserved each year for minority applicants, Bakke, whose academic record and test scores were better than those of nearly every admitted minority student, sued the medical school, charging racial discrimination.

In what ranks as one of the most splintered decisions ever rendered by the Supreme Court, the Justices in *Bakke* issued six separate opinions, none of which commanded a majority. On the basic matter before the Court, four Justices— William Rehnquist, John Paul Stevens, Potter Stewart, and Chief Justice Warren Burger—ruled that the two-tiered admissions program at the UC-Davis medical school was unconstitutional, while four others—Harry Blackmun, William Brennan, Thurgood Marshall, and Byron White—wanted to uphold it. Resolution of the case thus depended on the swing vote of Justice Lewis Powell.

In his own notoriously indecisive opinion, Powell found common ground with both sides. The admissions program at the UC-Davis medical school was, he agreed, plainly illegal, and had done an injustice to Allan Bakke. Though racial classifications were perhaps permissible in individual cases as a remedy for documentable discrimination, they could not be justified as an instrument for overcoming the effects of "societal" discrimination, "an amorphous concept of injury that may be ageless in its reach into the past." "Preferring members of one group for no reason other than race or ethnic origin," Powell wrote, "is discrimination for its own sake. This the Constitution forbids."

Trever. © 1995 by John Trever. Reprinted with permission.

At the same time, however, Powell endorsed the idea that colleges could take race into account in their admissions decisions without running afoul of the Constitution. The key, as he saw it, citing procedures then in use at Harvard College, was not to assign an inordinate weight to race or ethnicity but rather to treat them as modest "plus" factors, like having extraordinary leadership qualities or coming from an underrepresented region of the country. In selecting their students, universities had the right to consider such things because doing so furthered what was, to Powell's mind, an invaluable educational good: diversity. As he explained, "People do not learn very much when they are surrounded only by the likes of themselves."

For more than two decades, Justice Powell's attempt to split the difference in *Bakke* has been the only road map available to college administrators—and it has given them abundant room to maneuver. "The decision may have been a statesmanlike piece of jurisprudence," wrote the journalist Nicholas Lemann, a defender of affirmative action, in 1995, "but in admissions-office circles it is widely viewed as meaning that it's O.K. to reverse-discriminate"—that is, to discriminate in favor of minority candidates—"as long as you're not really obvious about it."

## Discrimination Under Wraps

At most selective public universities in the wake of *Bakke*, the need to keep reverse discrimination from being "really obvious" translated into an effort to keep it under wraps. This meant, above all, not releasing potentially embarrassing information about how admissions decisions were actually being made.

This is how it was, too, at the University of Michigan at Ann Arbor. There, not only were white and nonwhite applicants evaluated according to vastly different criteria, but, in contravention of the constitutional principle enunciated by Powell himself, a specific number of admission slots were set aside for minorities. But then, as Lemann recently related in the *New Yorker*, the facts were uncovered and documented in the mid-1990's by Carl Cohen, a professor of philosophy at the university and a long-time foe of racial preferences.

Thanks to the efforts of Cohen and others, Michigan was forced to revamp its admissions procedures. In 1998, the school introduced a new system, still in use in 2001, under which all applicants would be evaluated on a single 150-point scale—a scale, however, on which blacks and Hispanics would be automatically awarded an extra 20 points. Both sets of admissions procedures, the old and the new, were the target of the suit brought in 1997 by Jennifer Gratz and Patrick Hamacher, two white applicants who had been re-

131

jected by the Ann Arbor campus in favor, they argued, of less qualified minority students.

In deciding the case of *Gratz v. Bollinger* (Lee Bollinger being the president of the University of Michigan), Judge Patrick J. Duggan of the federal district court emphasized that his guiding light was Justice Powell's opinion in *Bakke*. This meant, in the first place, that the dual-track admissions program in use at Michigan when Gratz and Hamacher applied—in 1995 and 1997, respectively—did not pass constitutional muster. Reserving a set number of places for minorities, Duggan declared, was just the kind of invidious racial classification that Allan Bakke had confronted, and that the Supreme Court, with Powell's deciding vote, had struck down.

But the current admissions guidelines at Michigan were another matter altogether. These, Judge Duggan averred, not only embodied the sort of nuanced treatment of minority applicants that Powell had outlined, but they did so in the service of the very goal about which Powell had spoken with such evident enthusiasm. As Duggan himself put it, having a "racially and ethnically diverse student body produces significant educational benefits," and thus "constitutes a compelling government interest."

Nor did Judge Duggan simply assert the existence of these "significant educational benefits." His claim was supported, he wrote, by "solid evidence," in particular the research conducted at the University of Michigan's request by Patricia Gurin of the school's psychology department. According to Gurin's report, which Judge Duggan cited at length, a racially diverse campus was essential to achieving a range of important educational goals. It led students to "learn more and think in deeper, more complex ways"; it made them better able to understand "multiple perspectives" and less subject to "a problem termed 'group think,'" in which "group members mindlessly conform"; and, finally, it allowed them to "appreciate the common values and integrative forces that harness differences in pursuit of common ground."

For the friends of racial preferences in higher education, the importance of these claims cannot be exaggerated. After all, if preferences do serve an abiding educational purpose rather

132

than just a remedial one—if, that is, they benefit all students rather than just aggrieved minorities—the country's public universities may at long last win a reprieve from the hostile attention of the courts and, more important, a free hand in determining the racial composition of their student bodies.

## The "Diversity" Rationale

Is there, then, "solid evidence" of diversity's benefits? Take, to begin with, the report of the psychologist Patricia Gurin that was so impressive to Judge Duggan. As was pointed out in an amicus brief filed on behalf of the plaintiffs by the National Association of Scholars, Gurin's research is hardly a model of rigorous social science. Nowhere, for instance, does she provide a direct measure of the racial make-up of the universities in her analysis. Rather, she simply assumes that a school has grown more diverse if, over time, it has offered more courses in racial and ethnic studies.

What exactly this index of diversity is supposed to tell us is far from clear. At what level of racially mixed attendance do classes like "Introduction to Afro-American Studies" or "Chicana Literature" become sufficiently diverse to satisfy the criterion of diversity? And if such courses are attended only by blacks and Hispanics, can they still be said to contribute to the goal of imparting "multiple perspectives" to all students on campus? And what does the mere existence of such courses have to do with what actually happens in them? Gurin either does not know or cannot say—a serious shortcoming, one would think, in research purporting to show the benefits of racial preferences in creating diversity.

Still less persuasive is Gurin's claim that diversity, as defined by the presence of such classes, serves important educational ends. For this finding, it turns out, she relied not on independent assessments but, for the most part, on students' self-evaluations. Thus, it was the students themselves who concluded that their coursework in racial and ethnic studies had made them—in the vacuous and inimitable slogans of multiculturalism—"think in deeper, more complex ways" and learn to "harness [their] differences." Others may question whether this represents, as Gurin claims, an antidote to the problem of "group think," or is rather an example of it.

or evidence that the latter may be the case, one need
no further than a recent collection of "diary-like" essays
students at the law school of the University of California
at Berkeley. Asked to rate the health of the marketplace of
ideas at their multicultural law school, many of them readily
testified, in the words of the book's editor, that "race serves
as a proxy for opinion," and that diversity at the Berkeley law
school "is defined according to skin color rather than according to ideas."

Perhaps even more to the point, and tragically so in light
of the educational deficiencies that affirmative action often
serves to mask, Gurin's report failed to show—and, indeed,
seemed uninterested in finding—any link between diversity
and such traditional measures of academic achievement as
improved grades, test scores, and graduation rates. The existence of just such a link was, as it happens, a chief claim of
William G. Bowen and Derek Bok, former presidents respectively of Princeton and Harvard, in their 1998 book, *The
Shape of the River*, where it is cited as one of the justifications
for continued adherence to racial preferences.

Bowen and Bok said they saw nothing "disappointing" in
the graduation rates of the beneficiaries of affirmative action. But in order to arrive at this conclusion, as Stephan
Thernstrom and Abigail Thernstrom demonstrated in a
scathing review-article in *Commentary*, they had to overlook
the alarmingly high drop-out rate of students admitted under preferential quotas (for blacks at elite schools, 3.3 times
the white rate), and they also methodically downplayed the
no less alarming statistics on actual classroom performance.
Finally, on the related issue of whether, as advertised, diversity furthers interracial friendships, it turns out according to
the Thernstroms that the incidence of such friendships on
our nation's race-conscious campuses lags far behind the
norm for American society as a whole.

## Troubling Constitutional Questions

As for the constitutional issues at stake in *Gratz*, Judge Duggan was surely too quick to conclude that Justice Powell
would have come down in favor of the system now in use at
the University of Michigan. A scale that awards bonus points

to black and Hispanic applicants may be more subtle than a grid that simply sets them apart for separate consideration, but both provide a significant advantage on the basis of nothing other than surname and skin color. In the admissions process at Michigan, being a member of a minority group remains a good deal more than a modest "plus" factor.

More fundamentally, though, it is wholly unclear that Powell's endorsement of diversity as a justification for affirmative action deserves to carry any legal weight. Indeed, a principal conclusion of the Fifth Circuit's ruling in *Hopwood* in 1996 was that it does not. As that court noted, though Powell may have sympathized (to a degree) with the four Justices who wanted to uphold racial preferences, those same four Justices, for their part, declined to support his view of diversity; and so, of course, did the four Justices who voted to strike down the program at UC-Davis. What this means, as Carl Cohen noted shortly after the ruling in *Hopwood,* is that Powell's opinion "cannot bind lower courts, and may not be supposed to lay down the constitutional rules governing the way race can be used."

Indeed, the *Hopwood* judges made short work of the arguments so uncritically embraced by Duggan. The Supreme Court, they pointed out, has consistently held that race-based programs are acceptable only as a narrowly tailored remedy for the documented effects of discrimination. Diversity in higher education, by contrast, was not nearly so compelling a government interest; to the contrary, it raised troubling constitutional questions of its own. As the *Hopwood* court tartly observed:

> [T]he use of race in admissions for diversity in higher education contradicts, rather than furthers, the aims of equal protection. Diversity fosters, rather than minimizes, the use of race. It treats minorities as a group, rather than as individuals. It . . . may promote improper racial stereotypes, thus fueling racial hostility.

Moreover, the court in *Hopwood* understood that the effects of race-conscious admissions extend far beyond the campus gates. The pursuit of diversity for its own sake encourages Americans to use race as a stand-in for an individual's experiences, ideas, and outlook, sanctioning, as the court put it, "the mode of thought and behavior that underlies most prejudice and bigotry in modern America." Worse, affirmative action encourages minorities to think of their prospects as determined by their race, a view that has had a devastatingly subversive effect on the attitudes of many young blacks toward academic achievement.

Whether the ruling in *Gratz* will have any lasting impact may in the end be up to the Supreme Court. The Justices decided not to review *Hopwood* because the program in question at the University of Texas was discontinued. After the case from Michigan emerges from the appeals process, the Court will have its first opportunity in almost a quarter-century to rule directly on race-based admissions—and on the seemingly unshakable devotion of our universities to a pernicious doctrine that has been consistently rejected by the American people in opinion polls, that has rightly begun to come under the sanction of lower courts and voters alike, and that has injected more than a generation's worth of poison into the social air we breathe. One can only hope for the best.

# Periodical Bibliography

The following articles have been selected to supplement the diverse views presented in this chapter.

| | |
|---|---|
| William C. Bowen and Derek Bok | "The Proof Is in the Pudding," *Washington Post National Weekly Edition*, September 28, 1998. |
| James A. Buford Jr. | "Affirmative Action Works," *Commonweal*, June 19, 1998. |
| Roger Clegg | "Racial and Ethnic Preferences in Higher Education," *National Forum: The Phi Kappa Phi Journal*, Winter 1999. |
| Trevor W. Coleman | "Affirmative Action Wars," *Emerge*, March 1998. |
| *Commentary* | "Is Affirmative Action on the Way Out? Should It Be?" (symposium), March 1998. |
| Ward Connerly | "One Nation, Indivisible," *Hoover Digest*, Winter 2001. |
| Kenneth J. Cooper | "A Campus Diversity Experiment," *Washington Post National Weekly Edition*, April 10, 2000. |
| Nathan Glazer | "In Defense of Preference," *New Republic*, April 6, 1998. |
| *Issues and Controversies on File* | "Update: Affirmative Action," June 9, 2000. |
| Wilbert Jenkins | "Why We Must Retain Affirmative Action," *USA Today*, September 1999. |
| Amanda Ripley | "Yes, Your Race Still Matters," *Time*, October 23, 2000. |
| Thomas Sowell | "Misshapen Statistics on Racial Quotas," *American Spectator*, April 1999. |
| Shelby Steele | "We Shall Overcome—but Only Through Merit," *Wall Street Journal*, September 16, 1999. |
| Stephan Thernstrom and Abigail Thernstrom | "Racial Preferences: What We Now Know," *Commentary*, February 1999. |
| Barbara Whitaker | "Minority Rolls Rebound at University of California," *New York Times*, April 5, 2000. |

# CHAPTER 4

# How Can Society End Discrimination?

# Chapter Preface

Stopping discrimination is an ongoing challenge for Americans. Efforts to curb racism and sexism in the workplace, for example, seem to have mixed results. While affirmative action policies have expanded employment opportunities for women and minorities, a growing number of people believe that such policies create unfair hiring preferences based on race and gender. Moreover, the number of discrimination lawsuits filed by women and minorities has increased over the years. According to the Equal Employment Opportunity Commission (EEOC), in 1997 there were 36,419 race discrimination lawsuits that resulted in favorable rulings for plaintiffs—in comparison to 28,914 in 1991. Similarly, the number of favorable outcomes in sex discrimination lawsuits rose from 18,817 in 1991 to 32,836 in 1997. While these statistics could be seen as proof that more women and minorities are receiving well-deserved compensation for racism and sexism, they also suggest that race and gender based discrimination remains a serious problem in the workplace.

Many U.S. companies have tried to address such discrimination by adopting diversity-training programs. Diversity training became popular after a 1987 Labor Department report projected that after the year 2000, most new employees would be women and minorities. The goal of most of these programs has been to deter workplace racism and sexism by developing workers' appreciation of gender, ethnic, and racial differences. Diversity trainers use a number of tools—including discussions, films, games, and role-playing—to enhance workers' understanding of the problems faced by women and people of color. More than two-thirds of major U.S. companies run programs designed to stop sexual harassment, alleviate racial tensions, and reveal discriminatory practices.

In the 1990s, many analysts criticized diversity programs, claiming that they actually perpetuated stereotypes and failed to address discriminatory barriers to employee advancement. For example, workers often found that they would be "trained" to value the allegedly different work styles of women and minorities with negative stereotypes (for example, "women are emotional") restated as positive ones ("women are intuitive"). As commentator Gillian Flynn points out, "These procedures do little to foster individual respect. The goal is to allow each individual footing in the company, not to give all employees checklists so they can say, 'Hello, you're Hispanic, I am aware you may not start meetings on time. I value that approach.'"

A better way to conduct diversity training, many observers maintain, is through a technique known as "dialoguing." With dialoguing, employees engage in ongoing, thoughtful discussions about race, gender, class, and personality issues. According to community organizer Sanford Cloud Jr., "It starts with trained facilitators and people whose group identifications and life experiences differ. The facilitator keeps the exchange focused and helps participants get to the issues." Companies that adopt dialoguing often have groups of employees meet once a month for a year or more for cross-cultural discussion. The sustained nature of the dialogue gives employees the time, discipline, and comfort level to explore issues in depth; it also fosters respect for each participant's individuality, proponents contend.

While diversity programs have come under fire in recent years, many companies are likely to try new ways of counteracting discrimination rather than abandon diversity training altogether. In the following chapter, authors offer differing opinions on diversity training as well as other approaches to eliminating institutional discrimination.

VIEWPOINT

*"Community dialogue can be a way both to demonstrate and to strengthen our will to become active in the task of dismantling racism."*

# Diversity-Training Programs Are Productive

Andrea Ayvazian and Beverly Daniel Tatum

In the following viewpoint, diversity consultants Andrea Ayvazian and Beverly Daniel Tatum assert that diversity-training programs that promote dialogue between whites and people of color are an effective way to confront racial discrimination on a community level. Well-organized forums led by skilled facilitators can, in the authors' opinion, encourage honest, revealing, and empathetic discussion. Such dialogue, the authors contend, battles discrimination by helping people of different backgrounds to more fully understand each other as individuals. Ayvazian is the director of Communitas Incorporated, a nonprofit diversity-training organization, in Northampton, Massachusetts. Tatum is a psychology and education professor at Mount Holyoke College in South Hadley, Massachusetts.

As you read, consider the following questions:
1. In the authors' opinion, why do whites tend to be less aware of racial issues than people of color are?
2. According to the authors, why is it difficult for most white people to listen to and believe people of color?
3. In Ayvazian and Tatum's opinion, how do caucus groups assist the process of community dialogue?

From "Can We Talk?" by Andrea Ayvazian and Beverly Daniel Tatum, *Sojourners*, January/February 1996. Copyright © 1996 by *Sojourners*. Reprinted with permission.

A n African-American woman notices that as she enters a room full of friends and colleagues—all white—the conversation stops when she walks through the door. An African-American man is routinely followed by the local police as he drives through a suburban community on his way to work. When he tells his white colleagues at work, his story is met with disbelief.

These vignettes are representative of the many stories we have heard as a biracial team that has provided hundreds of anti-racism training seminars and consultations nationwide. We ask people—white and of color—to talk about a subject that folks are usually careful to avoid: race relations and racism in the United States today.

With the [O.J.] Simpson verdict and the Million Man March [a 1995 mass meeting of African-American men in Washington, D.C.] behind us, the desire to avoid potentially painful and difficult discussions has become even more intense. At the same time, many people are confused about why there is still such a deep racial divide in this country.

Recently in our travels, we have noticed that while people are reticent to discuss issues of race and racism in public, they pull us aside and ask us in whispered tones what we really think, or they explain their own theories to us behind closed doors. Even in these guarded conversations, we have been struck by a discernible change in tone. Suddenly, it seems, white people are seeing the racial divide as looming larger than before. Race, so often dismissed by white people as an insignificant factor in contemporary U.S. society, has acquired meaning—meaning that they were working hard to ignore. There seems to be a veiled sense of panic in their conversation.

## Racial Wounds

Because issues of injustice are always clearer from below, people of color have recognized the reality of racism for a very long time. But white America has enjoyed the dual luxuries of ignorance and denial. Many whites have claimed— with a misplaced sense of pride—that they did not see color in friends, students, neighbors, or colleagues. In order to avoid confronting the disease of racism, whites have clung to the myth of colorblindness. However, recent events have forced many whites to acknowledge that racism is still imbedded in the fabric of our society.

The nation is raw and divided—the racial wound is now more visible than it has been at any time since the civil rights movement and the urban riots of the 1960s. Just as we are hearing expressions of a quiet panic coming from whites in this country, the people of color we talk to are angry, and very cynical about white America's commitment to effecting significant change.

And yet, even against this backdrop of fear, anger, and cynicism, we believe that as a nation we have entered a period when the possibility for real change on the issue of racism is presenting itself. We believe that, as a people, we are at an important historical moment. The fact that racism has now surfaced so visibly once again gives us the opportunity to confront it directly, and to move forward in new and constructive ways.

Are we on the verge of a second wave of the civil rights movement? Maybe. We are unsure. What we are sure about is that we are hearing a level of concern, agitation, empowerment, and fear—along with a desire for dialogue surrounding the issue of racism that we have not heard in the last 20 years.

## The Need for Public Dialogue

If we are indeed at one of those rare . . . moments when there exists the possibility for a significant paradigm shift, what can we do to seize this moment and move toward race equity in this country?

We believe the greatest need exists on the community level: the need for deep, honest, and ongoing public dialogue on race and racism between white people and people of color conducted in safe settings and in a structured fashion. Due to the level of segregation in our society, most white adults only interact with people of color at their workplace (if at all); their neighborhoods, houses of worship, and social circles remain predominantly white.

When we say that we need public dialogue on the community level about issues of race, we do not mean social events that encourage friendly mixing and polite conversation (although those may be useful as well). The public gatherings we are referring to would be specifically for the purpose of discussing race and racism. They would, moreover, have clearly stated goals, such as: an enhanced understanding of the manifestations of cultural and institutional racism and their impact in one's own community; the creation of mutually beneficial coalitions across racial lines; and the empowerment of people of color and white allies to effect serious change.

We believe that these organized community dialogues need to be carefully structured, with a clear agenda hammered out in advance by white folks and people of color, and skillfully facilitated to create a level of safety that allows participants to speak openly—on the emotional as well as cognitive levels—without fear of reprisal.

---

## Cross-Cultural Dialogue

America needs dialogue. Most of us live and socialize in isolated communities, notwithstanding statistics indicating that our broader environments are increasingly diverse. It's no surprise that people often view themselves and those who are different through a homogenous lens, perpetuating stereotypes and bias. Structured dialogue can open that lens to reveal our hidden assumptions and suspicions about others. By sitting down and talking this talk, we become able to walk the walk of collaborators and community problem-solvers.

Cross-cultural dialogue is not a new concept, nor is it some obscure scientific endeavor too difficult for the ordinary person. It starts with trained facilitators and people whose group identifications and life experiences differ. The facilitator keeps the exchange focused and helps participants get to the issues.

Sanford Cloud Jr., *Christian Science Monitor*, March 5, 1998.

---

When planning a public forum to discuss racism in one's community, organizers must recognize that people of color and white people do not usually enter the dialogue with the same level of awareness or sophistication about these issues. People of color know a great deal about white America— they must, to function in this country. They also know a great deal about racism. In contrast, much of white America remains remarkably unaware of the lives, feelings, and hardships of people of color.

One of the most common questions asked by whites in our dismantling racism workshops is: What do I call them? Black or African American? Latino/a or Hispanic? Native American or Indian? And so on. Although no longer surprised by this question, we are dismayed by it because it is indicative of the degree of white people's insulation from communities of color.

Many people of color understand the power differential inherent in the three manifestations of racism: personal, cultural, and institutional. They view racism not as an individual issue but as a systemic problem. However, many white people still characterize racism as a virulent form of individual prejudice—they reduce the problem to what Peggy McIntosh calls "individual acts of meanness." They are unschooled in the systematic ways that racism has been institutionalized and are oblivious to the reality of privilege given automatically and invisibly to white people every single day.

Because it is almost inevitable that white people and people of color will begin any discussion of racism with vastly different perceptions of the problem, a public dialogue needs to begin with white people doing something for which they may have little practice: listening intently to people of color. Whites need to listen to the stories and the struggles of people of color in their own or surrounding communities. Not judge, debate, defend, solve, or critique—but listen. Through the simple act of listening, the subtle and pervasive nature of "neoracism"—the racism of the 1980s and 1990s—may become evident.

## Listening and Believing

However, listening itself will not reach hearts or change minds unless white people are encouraged to take another step that contradicts countless messages from their growing years, that is: to believe people of color. Although simple, this combination of listening and believing makes for a radical prescription.

Asking white people to listen to and to believe people of color sounds like an easy request. But, in our experience, whites almost invariably resist the idea, and deny that they don't believe people of color. Genuinely believing people of color requires that white people examine some of the messages, images, and cues received as children that taught them otherwise.

Most white people were not given overt messages in their growing years to doubt people of color, they simply absorbed the prevailing bias in society of white superiority. Consequently, whites learned to "second guess" people of color, to assume they were smarter, and to dismiss information that they heard from people of color that contradicted their own experience in the world. But, with modeling, guidance, and support, whites can be helped to listen with an open mind and an undefended and believing heart. Imagine the difference in our communities if white people started listening intently to people of color and believing that what they were hearing were actually true.

Unfortunately, most people have had few opportunities to witness the kind of open, honest, and mutually respectful dialogue that we envision. They do not know how to begin, are uncertain of how to challenge old behaviors and assumptions, and are afraid to let down their defenses.

We have found that both white people and people of color benefit when community dialogues on racism are cofacilitated by a biracial team willing to engage in frank dialogue between themselves as a model for the group. This modeling provides a concrete example of the level of trust and openness expected in the dialogue, and helps develop a sense of safety in the room.

Public dialogue of this nature seems to work best when people speak from their own experiences about their own lives. If participants make a commitment to an ongoing series of meetings, it is both effective and useful—for the reasons outlined above—to have the people of color speak first about their struggles and tell their stories. We have facilitated gatherings where people of color voluntarily responded to a set of questions presented by the facilitators. This structure gives the discussion a starting point and a sense of boundaries, and brings the dialogue to the personal and community level immediately.

## Caucus Groups

Many people of color are weary of educating white people about racism, and may not want to participate in such forums. People of color should be given full support if they decide that a public community dialogue where they would be speaking about their lives and struggles is not an event they choose to participate in for whatever reasons. The community dialogue should only include those people of color who feel they have something to gain as well as something to give, and who willingly choose to participate.

A helpful exercise that speaks directly to the twin issues of people of color continuously having to educate white folks and white folks often being less informed about race issues is meeting in caucus groups. This exercise involves subdividing by race and having the people of color meet separately with the facilitator of color and the white people meet with the white facilitator.

Caucuses provide folks with a safe place to explore difficult issues with members of their own group. The people of color may focus on empowerment issues and building a strong sense of group solidarity; the white people often struggle with their understanding of racism and how to be effective allies. We have found that, in this arrangement, people raise difficult questions that were previously unasked, members push one another, and confrontation is less threatening than in a racially mixed group. With skillful facilitation, caucus groups can accelerate the changes—greater openness, an ability truly to hear one another, and feelings of empathy—that are necessary for the community dialogue to be effective.

As is evident from our comments thus far, we believe in the power of *modeling* as a way to guide people into new behaviors. We have seen the tremendous impact that Cornel West and Michael Lerner have had as they crisscross the country modeling an open, honest, and respectful dialogue on black-Jewish relations. Maya Angelou and Elie Wiesel also share the same stage talking about victimization, empowerment, and building alliances across differences.

We feel that more public dialogues are needed that focus on black-white relations, or more generally, whites and people of color. We have imagined Angela Davis, bell hooks, or Toni Morrison teamed up with Morris Dees, Jimmy Carter, or Bill Bradley to discuss racism in America.

As a biracial team, we have taken part in just such an endeavor, engaging in an exchange we call "Women, Race, and Racism: A Dialogue in Black and White." People have expressed tremendous gratitude that we are able to talk about racism openly from our different perspectives and view this sort of an exchange as a concrete step in the journey toward justice. We encourage other biracial pairs to consider modeling for others a public dialogue about these issues; in our experience, it is an effective way to demonstrate the dialogue we hope to create on the community level.

We need to create public dialogues to move beyond polite and empty words, beyond slogans and accusations, and beyond the fears and hurts that close us off one from another. We must remember, however, that community dialogue is not an end in itself. It is an important and necessary beginning. Our goal is to move people along the continuum from uninformed to informed, from informed to concerned, and from concerned to active.

As a nation, we suffer from what Cornel West has called a "weak will to justice." In our experience, effective community dialogue can be a way both to demonstrate and to strengthen our will to become active in the task of dismantling racism. If we choose to invest the care and the time to organize the dialogue well, and if we decide to speak and to listen in a spirit of openness and trust, we can find avenues to join with one another to confront and dismantle racism in our own communities.

> *"The assault on individual identity was*
> *essential to the horror and inhumanity of*
> *Jim Crow laws. . . . It is no less inhuman*
> *when undertaken by 'diversity educators.'"*

# Diversity-Training Programs Are Counterproductive

Alan Charles Kors

Alan Charles Kors is a professor of history at the University of Pennsylvania and president of the Foundation for Individual Rights in Education. He is also the coauthor of *The Shadow University: The Betrayal of Liberty on America's Campuses*. In the following viewpoint, Kors denounces the diversity-training programs commonly found on today's college campuses. These programs, which attempt to curb various kinds of discrimination by making students more sensitive to racial, gender, class, and sexuality issues, amount to nothing more than political brainwashing, Kors maintains. All too often, student individuality and dignity is sacrificed to an allegedly "progressive" agenda that rejects independent thinking and perpetuates stereotypes.

As you read, consider the following questions:

1. What happens in the diversity-training film *Blue Eyed*, according to Kors?
2. In Kors's opinion, how does the sensitivity-training film *Skin Deep* exemplify Orwellian thought reform?
3. How does Denise Bynes categorize the "basic values" of various American ethnic groups, according to the author?

Excerpted from "Thought Reform 101," by Alan Charles Kors, *Reason*, March 2000. Copyright © 2000 by the Reason Foundation. Reprinted with permission.

At Wake Forest University in the fall of 1999, one of the few events designated as "mandatory" for freshman orientation was attendance at *Blue Eyed*, a filmed racism awareness workshop in which whites are abused, ridiculed, made to fail, and taught helpless passivity so that they can identify with "a person of color for a day." In Swarthmore College's dormitories, in the fall of 1998, first-year students were asked to line up by skin color, from lightest to darkest, and to step forward and talk about how they felt concerning their place in that line. Indeed, at almost all of our campuses, some form of moral and political re-education has been built into freshman orientation and residential programming. These exercises have become so commonplace that most students do not even think of the issues of privacy, rights, and dignity involved.

A central goal of these programs is to uproot "internalized oppression," a crucial concept in the diversity education planning documents of most universities. Like the Leninists' notion of "false consciousness," from which it ultimately is derived, it identifies as a major barrier to progressive change the fact that the victims of oppression have internalized the very values and ways of thinking by which society oppresses them. What could workers possibly know, compared to intellectuals, about what workers truly should want? What could students possibly know, compared to those creating programs for offices of student life and residence, about what students truly should feel? Any desire for assimilation or for individualism reflects the imprint of white America's strategy for racial hegemony.

## The Claims of Diversity Educators

In 1991 and 1992 both the *New York Times* and the *Wall Street Journal* published surveys of freshman orientations. The *Times* observed that "orientation has evolved into an intense . . . initiation" that involves "delicate subjects like . . . date rape [and] race relations, and how freshmen, some from small towns and tiny high schools, are supposed to deal with them." In recent years, public ridicule of "political correctness" has made academic administrators more circumspect about speaking their true minds, so one should listen carefully to the claims made for these programs before colleges began to spin their politically correct agendas.

Tony Tillman, in charge of a mandatory "Social Issues" orientation at Dartmouth, explained in the *Journal* that students needed to address "the various forms of 'isms': sexism, racism, classism," all of which were interrelated. Oberlin "educated" its freshmen about "differences in race, ethnicity, sexuality, gender, and culture," with separate orientations for blacks, Hispanics, gays and lesbians, and Americans of Asian descent. Columbia University sought to give its incoming students the chance "to reevaluate [and] learn things," so that they could rid themselves of "their own social and personal beliefs that foster inequality." Katherine Balmer, assistant dean for freshmen at Columbia, explained to the *Times* that "you can't bring all these people together . . . without some sort of training."

Greg Ricks, multicultural educator at Stanford (after similar stints at Dartmouth and Harvard), was frank about his agenda: "White students need help to understand what it means to be white in a multicultural community. . . . For the white heterosexual male who feels disconnected and marginalized by multiculturalism, we've got to do a lot of work here." Planning for New Student Week at Northwestern University, a member of the Cultural Diversity Project Committee explained to the *Weekly Northwestern Review* in 1989 that the committee's goal was "changing the world, or at least the way [undergraduates] perceive it." In 1993, Ana Maria Garcia, assistant dean of Haverford College, proudly told the *Philadelphia Inquirer* of official freshman dormitory programs there, which divided students into two groups: happy, unselfish Alphas and grim, acquisitive Betas. For Garcia, the exercise was wonderfully successful: "Students in both groups said the game made them feel excluded, confused, awkward, and foolish," which, for Garcia, accomplished the purpose of Haverford's program: "to raise student awareness of racial and ethnic diversity."

In the early 1990s, Bryn Mawr College shared its mandatory "Building Pluralism" program with any school that requested it. Bryn Mawr probed the most private experiences of every first-year student: difference and discomfort; racial, ethnic, and class experiences; sexual orientation; religious beliefs. By the end of this "orientation," students were devising "individual and collective action plans" for "breaking free" of "the cycle of oppression" and for achieving "new meaning" as "change agents." Although the public relations savvy of universities has changed since the early 1990s, these programs proliferate apace.

## Thought Reform 101

The darkest nightmare of the literature on power is George Orwell's *1984*, where there is not even an interior space of privacy and self. Winston Smith faces the ultimate and consistent logic of the argument that everything is political, and he can only dream of "a time when there were still privacy, love, and friendship, and when members of a family stood by one another without needing to know the reason."

Orwell did not know that as he wrote, Mao's China was subjecting university students to "thought reform," known also as "re-education," that was not complete until children had denounced the lives and political morals of their parents and emerged as "progressive" in a manner satisfactory to their trainers. In the diversity education film *Skin Deep*, a favorite in academic "sensitivity training," a white student in his third day of a "facilitated" retreat on race, with his name on the screen and his college and hometown identified, confesses his family's inertial Southern racism and, catching his breath, says to the group (and to the thousands of students who will see this film on their own campuses), "It's a tough choice, choosing what's right and choosing your family."

Political correctness is not the end of human liberty, because political correctness does not have power commensurate with its aspirations. It is essential, however, to understand those totalizing ambitions for what they are. O'Brien's re-education of Winston in *1984* went to the heart of such invasiveness. "We are not content with negative obedience. . . . When finally you surrender to us, it must be of your own free will." The Party wanted not to destroy the heretic but to "capture his inner mind." Where others were content to command "Thou shalt not" or "Thou shalt," O'Brien explains, "Our command is '*Thou art*.'" To reach that end requires "learning . . . understanding [and] acceptance," and the realization that one has no control even over one's inner soul. In *Blue Eyed*, the facilitator, Jane Elliott, says of those under her authority for the day, "A new reality is going to be created for these people." She informs everyone of the rules of the event: "You have no power, absolutely no power." By the end, broken and in tears, they see their own racist evil, and they love Big Sister.

The people devoted to remolding the inner lives of undergraduates are mostly kind and often charming individuals. At the Fourth Annual National Conference on People of Color in Predominantly White Institutions, held at and sponsored by the University of Nebraska last October, faculty and middle-level administrators of student life from around the country complained and joked about their low budgets, inadequate influence, and herculean tasks.

Their papers and interviews reveal an ideologically and humanly diverse crowd, but they share certain assumptions and beliefs, most of which are reasonable subjects for debate, but none of which should provide campuses with freshman agendas: America is an unjust society. Drop-out rates for students of color reflect a hostile environment and a lack of institutional understanding of identity and culture. What happens in the classroom is inadequate preparation for thinking correctly about justice and oppression.

They also share views that place us directly on the path of thought reform: White students desperately need formal "training" in racial and cultural awareness. The moral goal of such training should override white notions of privacy and individualism. The university must become a therapeutic and political agent of progressive change.

## A Political Re-Education

Handouts at the Nebraska conclave illustrated this agenda. Irma Amirall-Padamsee, the associate dean of student relations and the director of multicultural affairs at Syracuse University, distributed the Office of Multicultural Affairs' brochure. Its "philosophy" presupposes that students live "in a world impacted by various oppression issues," including "racism." "OMA's role," it announced, "is to provide the . . .

leadership needed to encourage our students . . . to grow into individuals willing to take a proactive stance against oppression in all its shapes."

Molly Tovar, who has done this sort of work both at the University of Oklahoma and at Oklahoma State University, passed out a 22-page guide she co-authored, "How to Build and Implement a Comprehensive Diversity Plan." The guide explains the three "kinds of attitudes" that agents of cultural change will face: "The Believers," who are "cooperative; excited; participative; contributive"; "The Fence Straddlers," who are "suspicious; observers; cautious; potentially open-minded"; and "The Skeptics," who are "critical; passive aggressive; isolated; traditional."

## Attacking Reason and Individualism

The multiculturalists assert that their sensitivity sessions are simply a way of achieving "cultural understanding" and "diversity." The sessions are nothing of the sort. They are a frontal assault on the guiding principles of Western civilization: reason and individualism. Indeed, the multiculturalists proudly proclaim that, for example, "logic and objectivity are white male values" and "blacks know through rhythm." At its core, multiculturalism is a mish-mash of racial collectivism, antirationalism, and a mystical faith in the wonders of ethnicity. The sensitivity sessions are simply a crude method of foisting these beliefs on generally captive audiences.

Nicholas Damask and James Damask, *World & I*, November 1994.

Ronnie Wooten, of Northern Illinois University, distributed a handout, "Inclusive Classroom Matters." It adapts a variety of common academic sources on multiculturalism, including a set of "guidelines" on how to "facilitate learning about those who are different from you." The students in this "inclusive classroom" would have to abandon what might be their sincere inner beliefs, replacing them with such professions of faith as "We will assume that people (both the groups we study and the members of the class) always do the best that they can." The guidelines make it clear that one may not restrict one's changes to the intellectual: "We will address the emotional as well as the cognitive content of the course material. We will work to break down the fears that prohibit communication."

Sharon Ulmar, assistant to the chancellor for diversity and equal opportunity at the University of Nebraska at Omaha, handed out a flyer titled "Can [A] Diversity Program Create Behavior Changes?" Her program's mode of self-evaluation was to measure "the number of participants that took action based upon the awareness they learned from [the] program." Among the units of "awareness" successfully acquired were the following (some of which surely might strike one as more problematic than others): "gays and lesbians no different than [sic] others"; "handicap accessibility is for those who are handicaped [sic]"; "difficult to make a decision about own beliefs when others are watching"; "module allowed participant to witness subtle behaviors instead of hearing about it"; and the ineffably tautological "understanding commonalities of each individual may be similar to yours."

Denise Bynes, program coordinator for Adelphi University's Center for African-American Studies Programs, distributed a "Conflict Resolution Styles Questionnaire" for students, all of whom are to be categorized at the end as one of the following: "competing, avoiding, accommodating, compromising, and collaborating." The handout also presents the "basic values" of each American ethnic group. For white Americans, these are "Freedom/liberty/privacy; equality/fairness; achievement/success; individualism/self-interest; economical use of time; comfort." For African-Americans, "Ethnic pride, heritage, history; kinship bonds/family/ motherhood; equality/fairness; achievement; respect; religion/spirituality." For Asian-Americans, "Reciprocal social duties; self-control/courtesy/dignity; devotion to parents; tradition (family, culture, the past); duty/hard work/diligence." Each group also has its own particular "overview" of nature, logic, time, society, and interpersonal relationships. Whites wish to "control" nature, for example; Hispanics, to live in "harmony" with it; blacks, to "overcome" it; and Asians, to "be adjusted to" and "accept" it. Whites are "rational, logical, analytical"; Hispanics, "rational, ethical"; blacks, "allegorical and synthetical"; and Asians, "intuitive, holistic, tolerate inconsistencies."

According to a formal presentation by Bynes and her colleague at Adelphi, Hinda Adele Barlaz, all of these materials were acquired during "training" by the U.S. Department of Justice Community Relations Service, a program so effective that "it was very hard to get any of the other white members of the committee [Barlaz was white] to go for the training that the Department of Justice provided free of charge. The white members of the [Adelphi Prejudice Reduction] Committee had been so alienated by the training that they didn't want to go back."

## Mandatory Sensitivity Training

What do these presenters in Nebraska, typical of those now governing offices of student life and residence, believe about the re-education of our college students? The keynote speaker at the conference was Carlos Muñoz, professor of ethnic studies at the University of California at Berkeley. He explains in an interview that to create an appropriate environment on campus, one has "to do as much outreach as possible away from the classroom, into the dorms, into the places where students live." Such work should begin during freshman orientation, continue throughout a college experience, and be mandatory.

Amirall-Padamsee from Syracuse argues that "students of color need to be nurtured as insightful leaders of our community" and that "they must be formally trained in anti-oppression theory and related skill building." "White students," in turn, "have to be trained as allies in change." (*Ally* is a code word in sensitivity training circles. As the "diversity facilitator" Hugh Vasquez of the Todos Institute explains in a widely used manual, an "ally" is someone from "the dominant group" who is aware of and articulates his unmerited privilege and who intervenes on behalf of mistreated groups.)

The goal of such training, according to Amirall-Padamsee, is "to produce graduates who are individuals committed to educational and social justice, and not just a tolerance of, but a validating of difference." To accomplish that she says, "we need to define and implement ways to translate education to behavioral change." In addition, she boasts, she has access to federal work-study funds, and she uses that position—and her capacity to dismiss people—"to try to make a positive change in the way that the student is thinking."

Tovar, formerly of Oklahoma State University and now at the University of Oklahoma, declares in an interview at the conference that "at OSU we have all kinds of sensitivity training." She describes an incident involving fraternity brothers who had been disrespectful of Native American culture: They ended up "incredibly emotional. . . . These fraternity kids broke down." OSU also has mandatory multicultural freshman orientation sessions.

Bynes, also the co-chairman of the Prejudice Reduction Committee at Adelphi University, says the committee's emphasis is on training individuals how to interact "with a diverse student body," with "separate training for students . . . [and] special sessions on student leadership training." This "cultural and racial awareness training would benefit all members of the Adelphi community, both in their university and personal lives." The committee would get people to talk about "'what I like about being so-and-so,' 'what I dislike about being so-and-so,' and 'the first time I encountered prejudice,'" all exercises that the facilitators had been shown and had experienced in their own "training" by the Justice Department.

Bynes is a kind, accomplished, candid, and well-meaning woman. As she explains, "White people must have . . . sensitivity training . . . so that they can become aware of white privilege." Mandatory sensitivity training ideally should include both students and faculty, but "there are things that we can't dictate to the faculty because of the fact that they have a union."

## An Assault on Individual Identity

There are painful ironies in these attempts at thought reform. Individual identity lies at the heart of both dignity and the flourishing of an ethnically heterogeneous society. Black students on American campuses rightly decry any tendency of university police to stop students based on race. Their objections are not statistical but moral: One is an individual, not an instance of blood or appearance. The assault on individual identity was essential to the horror and inhumanity of Jim Crow laws, of apartheid, and of the Nuremberg Race Laws. It is no less inhuman when undertaken by "diversity educators."

From the Inquisition to the political use of Soviet psychiatry, history has taught us to recoil morally from the violation of the ultimate refuges of self-consciousness, conscience, and private beliefs. The song of the "peat bog soldiers," sent by the Nazis to work until they died, was *"Die Gedanken sind frei,"* "Thoughts Are Free," for that truly is the final atom of human liberty. No decent society or person should pursue another human being there. Our colleges and universities do so routinely. . . .

Even traditionalist campuses now permit the ideologues in their offices of student life to pursue individuals into the last inner refuge of free men and women and to turn students over to trainers who want them to change "within themselves." This is a return of *in loco parentis*, with a power unimagined in prior ages by the poor souls who only tried to keep men and women from sleeping with each other overnight. It is the university standing not simply in the place of parents but in the place of private conscience, identity, and belief.

## "Getting Inside" American Students

From the evidence, most students tune it out, just as most students at most times generally have tuned out abuses of power and diminutions of liberty. One should not take heart from that. Where students react, it is generally with an anger that, ironically and sadly, exacerbates the balkanization of our universities. The more social work we bring to our colleges and universities, the more segregated they become, and in the classifieds of the *Chronicle of Higher Education* during the last few years, colleges and universities by the hundreds have advertised for individuals to oversee "diversity education," "diversity training," and "sensitivity training."

Orwell may have been profoundly wrong about the totalitarian effects of high technology, but he understood full well how the authoritarians of the twentieth century had moved from the desire for outer control to the desire for inner control. He understood that the new age sought to overcome what, in Julia's terms, was the ultimate source of freedom for human beings: "They can't get inside you." Our colleges and universities hire trainers to "get inside" American students.

Thought reform is making its way inexorably to an office near you. If we let it occur at our universities and accept it passively in our own domains, then a people who defeated totalitarians abroad will surrender their dignity, privacy, and conscience to the totalitarians within.

"*If we really wish to end the scourge of
racial profiling, we must address its roots:
drug laws that encourage police to consider
members of broad groups as probable
criminals.*"

# Racial Profiling Should Be Eliminated

Gene Callahan and William Anderson

In the following viewpoint, Gene Callahan and William Anderson argue that the national focus on the "war on drugs" causes police to unfairly investigate minorities and engage in racial profiling. To maximize drug arrests, police target minorities based on the statistical probability that they are more likely than whites to be carrying drugs. This practice, the authors explain, violates the basic legal principle that individuals should be treated equally until there is evidence of criminal activity. Police should concentrate on solving known crimes rather than creating dragnets to catch possible suspects, they conclude. Callahan is a freelance writer. Anderson is an assistant professor of economics at Frostburg State University in Maryland.

As you read, consider the following questions:
1. How much is spent annually on the war on drugs, according to Callahan and Anderson?
2. How do the authors define "case probability" and "class probability"?
3. In the authors' view, in what way could banning racial profiling without examining its causes hinder police work?

W hy are police targeting minorities for traffic stops?
It is early in the morning, and the well-dressed young African-American man driving his Ford Explorer on I-75 sees the blue lights of the Georgia State Patrol car behind him. The officer pulls behind the sport utility vehicle and the young man's heart begins to sink.

He is on his way to Atlanta for a job interview. The stop, ostensibly for speeding, should not take long, he reasons, as the highway patrol officer walks cautiously toward the Explorer. But instead of simply asking for a driver's license and writing a speeding ticket, the trooper calls for backup. Another trooper soon arrives, his blue lights flashing as well.

The young man is told to leave his vehicle, as the troopers announce their intention to search it. "Hey, where did you get the money for something like this?" one trooper asks mockingly while he starts the process of going through every inch of the Explorer. Soon, an officer pulls off an inside door panel. More dismantling of the vehicle follows. They say they are looking for drugs, but in the end find nothing. After ticketing the driver for speeding, the two officers casually drive off. Sitting in his now-trashed SUV, the young man weeps in his anger and humiliation.

## Daily Occurrences

Unmotivated searches like this are daily occurrences on our nation's highways, and blacks and white liberals have been decrying the situation for several years. Many conservatives, on the other hand, dismiss such complaints as the exaggerations of hypersensitive minorities. Or they say that if traffic cops do in fact pull over and search the vehicles of African Americans disproportionately, then such "racial profiling" is an unfortunate but necessary component of modern crime fighting.

The incident described above should give pause to those who think that racial profiling is simply a bogus issue cooked up by black leaders such as Al Sharpton and Jesse Jackson to use as another publicity tool. One of us teaches in an MBA program that enrolls a fairly large number of African Americans, and the story comes from one of our students. Indeed, during class discussions, all of the black men and many of the black women told stories of having their late-model cars pulled over and searched for drugs.

While incidents of racial profiling are widely deplored today, there is little said about the actual root cause of the phenomenon. The standard explanations for racial profiling focus on institutional racism, but that idea runs contrary to the sea change in social attitudes that has taken place over the last four decades. On the contrary, the practice of racial profiling grows from a trio of very tangible sources, all attributable to the War on Drugs, that $37 billion annual effort on the part of local, state, and federal lawmakers and cops to stop the sale and use of "illicit" substances. The sources include the difficulty in policing victimless crimes in general and the resulting need for intrusive police techniques; the greater relevancy of this difficulty given the intensification of the drug war since the 1980s; and the additional incentive that asset forfeiture laws give police forces to seize money and property from suspects. Since the notion of scaling back, let alone stopping, the drug war is too controversial for most politicians to handle, it's hardly surprising that its role in racial profiling should go largely unacknowledged.

## The Practice of Racial Profiling

Although there is no single, universally accepted definition of "racial profiling," we're using the term to designate the practice of stopping and inspecting people who are passing through public places—such as drivers on public highways or pedestrians in airports or urban areas—where the reason for the stop is a statistical profile of the detainee's race or ethnicity. . . .

Although some observers claim that racial profiling doesn't exist, there is an abundance of stories and statistics that document the practice. One case where law enforcement officers were particularly bold in their declaration of intent involved U.S. Forest Service officers in California's Mendocino National Forest [in the year 2000]. In an attempt to stop marijuana growing, forest rangers were told to question all Hispanics whose cars were stopped, regardless of whether pot was actually found in their vehicles. Tim Crews, the publisher of the *Sacramento Valley Mirror*, a biweekly newspaper, published a memo he'd gotten from a federal law enforcement officer. The memo told park rangers "to develop prob-able cause for stop . . . if a vehicle stop is conducted and no marijuana is located and the vehicle has Hispanics inside, at a minimum we would like all individuals FI'd [field interro-gated]." A spokeswoman for Mendocino National Forest called the directive an "unfortunate use of words."

The statistics are equally telling. Consider *Crises of the Anti-Drug Effort, 1999*, a report by Chad Thevenot of the Criminal Justice Policy Foundation, a group that monitors abuses of the American legal system. Thevenot writes: "76 percent of the motorists stopped along a 50-mile stretch of I-95 by Maryland's Special Traffic Interdiction Force (STIF) were black, according to an Associated Press com-puter analysis of car searches from January through September 1995. . . . Blacks constitute 25 percent of Mary-land's population, and 20 percent of Marylanders with driver's licenses." As this story was being written, New Jer-sey was holding hearings on racial profiling, and one state police investigator testified that 94 percent of the motorists stopped in one town were minorities.

Minorities are not only more likely to be stopped than whites, but they are also often pressured to allow searches of their vehicles, and they are more likely to allow such searches. In March, the *New York Times* reported that a 1997 investigation by New Jersey police of their own practices found that "turnpike drivers who agreed to have their cars searched by the state police were overwhelmingly black and Hispanic."

## Sensible Technique?

Some commentators, such as John Derbyshire in *National Review*, have defended racial profiling as nothing more than sensible police technique, where police employ the laws of probability to make the best use of their scarce resources in attacking crime. As Derbyshire put it in his February [2001] story, "In Defense of Racial Profiling," the police engage in the practice for reasons of simple efficiency: "A policeman who concentrates a disproportionate amount of his limited time and resources on young black men is going to uncover far more crimes—and therefore be far more successful in his career—than one who biases his attention toward, say, middle-aged Asian women."

George Will, in an April 19, [2001], *Washington Post* column, contends that the use of race as a criterion in traffic stops is fine, as long as it is just "one factor among others in estimating criminal suspiciousness." Similarly, Jackson Toby, a professor of sociology at Rutgers, argued in a 1999 *Wall Street Journal* op-ed that, "If drug traffickers are disproportionately black or Hispanic, the police don't need to be racist to stop many minority motorists; they simply have to be efficient in targeting potential drug traffickers."

Clayton Searle, president of the International Narcotics Interdiction Association, writes in a report, *Profiling in Law Enforcement*, "Those who purport to be shocked that ethnic groups are overrepresented in the population arrested for drug courier activities must have been in a coma for the last twenty years. The fact is that ethnic groups control the majority of the drug trade in the United States. They also tend to hire as their underlings and couriers others of their same group." (Searle's report is available at www.inia.org/whats-new.htm#Proflling.)

## Case Probability vs. Class Probability

The stories and statistics that draw outrage tend to share two common elements: They involve a search for drugs and the prospect of asset forfeiture. These types of investigations have led police from the solid ground of "case probability" to the shifting sands of "class probability" in their quest for probable cause. Once police are operating on the basis of class probability, there is a strong claim that certain groups of people are being denied equal protection under the law.

Case probability describes situations where we comprehend some factors relevant to a particular event, but not all such factors. It is used when a doctor tells a patient, "Given your lifestyle, you'll probably be dead in five years." Class probability refers to situations where we know enough about a class of events to describe it using statistics, but nothing about a particular event other than the fact that it belongs to the class in question. Class probability is being used when an insurance company estimates that a man who is 40 today will probably live to be, on average, about 80. The insurance company is not making any statement about the particular circumstances of any particular man, but merely generalizing about the class of 40-year-old men.

POLICE QUIZ: Which car would you pull over first?

ANSWER: C. The experienced officer will notice the driver is black, fitting the profile of a likely drug dealer.

Anderson. © 1989 by Kirk Anderson. Reprinted by permission.

This distinction helps us to differentiate two ways of using information about race or ethnicity in a police investigation. As an example of the first type, employing case probability, consider a mugging victim who has told the police that her mugger was a young Asian man. Here, it is quite understandable that the group of suspects investigated will not "look like America." There is no sense in forcing the police to drag in proportional numbers of whites, blacks, women, and so on, proving that they have interrogated a representative population sample of their city, before they can arrest an Asian fellow. No, their investigation should clearly focus on young Asian men. . . .

But when we turn our attention to the type of racial profiling that occurred on the highways of Maryland and New Jersey, or that is described in the Forest Service memo, we find a very different phenomenon, one where investigations proceeded on the basis of class probability. Here, before having evidence of a particular crime, police set out intending to investigate a high proportion of people of some particular race, ethnic group, age group, or so on. Their only justification is that by doing so, they increase their chances of discovering some crimes.

Additionally, there is a fundamental difference between the type of crime, such as the mugging example above, that is usually investigated by gathering evidence about a known crime, and narrowing the search based on such evidence, and the type investigated by looking in as many places as possible to see if one can find a crime. The first type of crime generally has a victim, and the police are aware of a specific crime that has been committed. The crime is brought to the attention of the police by a complainant, even if the complainant is a corpse.

George Will, in his defense of current police practice, points out: "Police have intelligence that in the Northeast drug-shipping corridor many traffickers are Jamaicans favoring Nissan Pathfinders." This is quite a different situation than having intelligence that a particular Jamaican robbed a store and escaped in a Pathfinder. If you are a law-abiding Jamaican who by chance owns a Pathfinder, you frequently will find yourself under police surveillance, even though the police have no evidence about any particular crime involving any particular Jamaican in a Pathfinder.

## The Cost of Class Probability

We could not have any effective law enforcement without allowing some scope for case probability. If your twin brother robs a bank in your hometown, it does not seem to be a civil rights issue if the police stop you on the street for questioning. When the police discover their mistake, they should apologize and make you whole for any damages you have suffered. Such an event, while unfortunate, is simply a byproduct of attempting to enforce laws in a world of error-prone human beings possessing less-than-perfect knowledge. It will be a rare event in law-abiding citizens' lives, and it is highly unlikely that such people will come to feel that they are being targeted.

However, the use of class probability in police investigations is correctly regarded with extreme suspicion, as it violates a basic principle of justice: The legal system should treat all citizens equally, until there is specific, credible evidence that they have committed a crime. In the cases we've been discussing, we can say that the odds that any particular young black or Hispanic man will be hassled by the police are much higher than for a white man who, aside from his race, is demographically indistinguishable from him. These minority men, no matter how law-abiding they are, know that they will be investigated by the police significantly more often than other citizens who are not members of their racial group. The social cost of the alienation produced by this situation cannot, of course, be measured, but common sense tells us that it must be great.

As important, in the majority of "crimes" that such stops discover, there is no third party whose rights have been violated, who can step forward and bring the crime to the attention of the police. To discover victimless crimes, investigators must become intrusive and simply poke around wherever they can, trying to see if they can uncover such a crime. When someone drives a few pounds of marijuana up I-95 from seller to buyer, who will come forward and complain? It's not merely that, as in the cases of robbery or murder, the perpetrator may try to hide his identity, but that the "crime" has no victim. . . .

## Drug War Profiling

If police have a goal of maximizing drug arrests, they may indeed find that they can achieve this most easily by focusing on minorities. Blacks on I-95 in Maryland, for instance, had a significantly higher initial propensity to carry drugs in the car than did whites. "Racial Bias in Motor Vehicle Searches: Theory and Evidence," a 1999 study by University of Pennsylvania professors John Knowles, Nicola Persico, and Petra Todd, shows that despite the fact that blacks were stopped three-and-a-half times more than whites, they were as likely to be carrying drugs. But this doesn't mean their propensity to carry is the same. If we assume that the high likelihood of being stopped reduces some blacks' willingness to carry drugs, then if not for the stops, they would have been carrying proportionally much more than whites. The Penn professors conclude they are displaying what they call "statistical discrimination" (i.e., the police are operating on the basis of class probability) rather than racial prejudice. Perhaps more to the point, they conclude that the police are primarily motivated by a desire to maximize drug arrests.

Some racial profiling defenders agree that the drug war bears a large part of the blame for racial profiling. "Many of the stop-and-search cases that brought this matter into the headlines were part of the so-called war on drugs," writes Derbyshire. "The police procedures behind them were ratified by court decisions of the 1980s, themselves mostly responding to the rising tide of illegal narcotics." But Derbyshire dismisses the argument that racial profiling is chiefly a by-product of the drug war. He contends that even if drugs were legalized tomorrow, the practice would continue.

He is confusing the two forms of police procedure we have outlined above. The practice of laying out broad dragnets to see what turns up would almost entirely disappear but for the attempt to stamp out drug trafficking and use. Derbyshire, to bolster his case, cites the fact that in 1997, "Blacks, who are 13 percent of the U.S. population, comprised 35 percent of those arrested for embezzlement." This statistic would be useful if he were defending the fact that 35 percent of those investigated for embezzling that year were black. But does Derbyshire believe that stopping random blacks on an interstate highway is catching very many embezzlers? Or that, absent the drug war, cops would start searching cars they pull over for embezzled funds? . . .

## This Is Your Law Enforcement on Drugs

In the panic created by the drug war, our traditional liberties have been eroded. Rather than regarding case probability as a necessary component of probable cause for searches or seizures, the American law enforcement system has now come to accept class probability as sufficient justification for many intrusions.

Unfortunately, the current protests against racial profiling are not addressing the root causes of the practice. Politicians, eager to please voters, have created potentially greater problems by trying to suppress the symptoms. As John Derbyshire points out, the laws rushed onto the books to end racial profiling result in severe obstacles to police officers attempting to investigate serious crimes. He notes, "In Philadelphia, a federal court order now requires police to fill out both sides of an 8½-by-11 sheet on every citizen contact." Unless our solution to this problem addresses its cause, we will be faced with the choice of either hindering important police work or treating some of our citizens, based on characteristics (race, age, and so on) completely beyond their control, in a manner that is patently unfair.

If we really wish to end the scourge of racial profiling, we must address its roots: drug laws that encourage police to consider members of broad groups as probable criminals. We must redirect law enforcement toward solving specific, known crimes using the particular evidence available to them about that crime. . . . It should be obvious that there's something nutty about a legal system that assumes suspects in murder, robbery, and rape cases are innocent until a trial proves otherwise, but assumes that a landscaper carrying some cash is guilty of drug trafficking.

Drugs, prohibitionists commonly point out, can damage a user's mind. They apparently can have the same effect on the minds of law enforcement officials.

*"The campaign to ban racial profiling is . . .
part of [a] large, broad-fronted assault on
common sense."*

# Racial Profiling Should Not Be Banned

John Derbyshire

Racial profiling—the practice of relying on race to identify
potential criminal suspects—has been widely condemned as
a form of discrimination by politicians and social analysts. In
the following viewpoint, *National Review* commentator John
Derbyshire offers a defense of racial profiling. He argues
that since a significantly high percentage of blacks commit
crimes, law enforcement officers are simply using common
sense when they disproportionately stop and search African
Americans. Banning racial profiling only leads to a decline in
the efficiency of police work and an increase in racial division and mistrust. Derbyshire maintains that police should
be allowed to use any predictable indicators of criminality,
including race, in fighting crime.

As you read, consider the following questions:
1. When did racial profiling first become a popular bone of
   contention, according to Derbyshire?
2. In the author's opinion, what is the primary function of
   stereotypes?
3. What statistic does Derbyshire point to as proof that
   blacks and Hispanics commit crimes at higher rates than
   whites do?

"Racial profiling" has become one of the shibboleths of our time. Anyone who wants a public career in the United States must place himself on record as being against it. Thus, ex-senator John Ashcroft, on the eve of his confirmation hearings: "It's wrong, inappropriate, shouldn't be done." During the vice-presidential debate in October 2000, moderator Bernard Shaw invited the candidates to imagine themselves black victims of racial profiling. Both made the required ritual protestations of outrage. Lieberman: "I have a few African-American friends who have gone through this horror, and you know, it makes me want to kind of hit the wall, because it is such an assault on their humanity and their citizenship." Cheney: "It's the sense of anger and frustration and rage that would go with knowing that the only reason you were stopped . . . was because of the color of your skin. . . ." In the strange, rather depressing, pattern these things always follow nowadays, the American public has speedily swung into line behind the Pied Pipers: Gallup reports that 81 percent of the public disapproves of racial profiling.

All of which represents an extraordinary level of awareness of, and hostility to, and even passion against ("hit the wall . . .") a practice that, up to about five years ago, practically nobody had heard of. It is, in fact, instructive to begin by looking at the history of this shibboleth.

## The History of "Racial Profiling"

To people who follow politics, the term "racial profiling" probably first registered when Al Gore debated Bill Bradley at New York's Apollo Theatre in February 2000. Here is Bradley, speaking of the 1999 shooting of African immigrant Amadou Diallo by New York City police: "I . . . think it reflects . . . racial profiling that seeps into the mind of someone so that he sees a wallet in the hand of a white man as a wallet, but a wallet in the hand of a black man as a gun. And we—we have to change that. I would issue an executive order that would eliminate racial profiling at the federal level."

Nobody was unkind enough to ask Sen. Bradley how an executive order would change what a policeman sees in a dark lobby in a dangerous neighborhood at night. Nor was anyone so tactless as to ask him about the case of LaTanya

Haggerty, shot dead in June 1999 by a Chicago police-woman who mistook her cell phone for a handgun. The policewoman was, like Ms. Haggerty, black.

Al Gore, in that debate at the Apollo, did successfully, and famously, ambush Bradley by remarking that: "You know, racial profiling practically began in New Jersey, Senator Bradley." In true Clinton-Gore fashion, this is not true, but it is sort of true. "Racial profiling" the thing has been around for as long as police work, and is practiced everywhere. "Racial profiling" the term did indeed have its origins on the New Jersey Turnpike in the early 1990s. The reason for the prominence of this rather unappealing stretch of expressway in the history of the phenomenon is simple: The turnpike is the main conduit for the shipment of illegal drugs and other contraband to the great criminal marts of the Northeast.

The career of the term "racial profiling" seems to have begun in 1994, but did not really take off until April 1998, when two white New Jersey state troopers pulled over a van for speeding. As they approached the van from behind, it suddenly reversed towards them. The troopers fired eleven shots from their handguns, wounding three of the van's four occupants, who were all black or Hispanic. The troopers, James Kenna and John Hogan, subsequently became poster boys for the "racial profiling" lobbies, facing the same indignities, though so far with less serious consequences, as were endured by the Los Angeles policemen in the Rodney King case: endless investigations, double jeopardy, and so on.

And a shibboleth was born. News-media databases list only a scattering of instances of the term "racial profiling" from 1994 to 1998. In that latter year, the number hit double digits, and thereafter rose quickly into the hundreds and thousands. Now we all know about it, and we are, of course, all against it.

## Only One Factor

Well, not quite all. American courts—including the U.S. Supreme Court—are not against it. Jurisprudence on the matter is pretty clear: So long as race is only one factor in a generalized approach to the questioning of suspects, it may be considered. And of course, pace Candidate Cheney, it always is only one factor. I have been unable to locate any statistics on the point, but I feel sure that elderly black women are stopped by the police much less often than are young white men.

Even in the political sphere, where truth-telling and independent thinking on matters of race have long been liabilities, there are those who refuse to mouth the required pieties. Alan Keyes, when asked by Larry King if he would be angry with a police officer who pulled him over for being black, replied: "I was raised that everything I did represented my family, my race, and my country. I would be angry with the people giving me a bad reputation."

Practically all law-enforcement professionals believe in the need for racial profiling. In an article on the topic for the *New York Times Magazine* in June 1999, Jeffrey Goldberg interviewed Bernard Parks, chief of the Los Angeles Police Department. Parks, who is black, asked rhetorically of racial profiling: "Should we play the percentages? . . . It's common sense." Note that date, though. This was pretty much the latest time at which it was possible for a public official to speak truthfully about racial profiling. Law-enforcement professionals were learning the importance of keeping their thoughts to themselves. Four months before the Goldberg piece saw print, New Jersey state-police superintendent Carl Williams, in an interview, said that certain crimes were associated with certain ethnic groups, and that it was naive to think that race was not an issue in policing—both statements, of course, perfectly true. Supt. Williams was fired the same day by Gov. Christie Todd Whitman.

## The Truth About Stereotypes

Like other race issues in the U.S., racial profiling is a "tadpole," with an enormous black head and a long but comparatively inconsequential brown, yellow, and red tail. While Hispanic, "Asian-American," and other lesser groups have taken up the "racial profiling" chant with gusto, the crux of the matter is the resentment that black Americans feel toward the attentions of white policemen. By far the largest number of Americans angry about racial profiling are law-abiding black people who feel that they are stopped and questioned because the police regard all black people with undue suspicion. They feel that they are the victims of a negative stereotype.

They are. Unfortunately, a negative stereotype can be correct, and even useful. I was surprised to find, when researching this article, that within the academic field of social psychology there is a large literature on stereotypes, and that much of it—an entire school of thought—holds that stereotypes are essential life tools. On the scientific evidence, the primary function of stereotypes is what researchers call "the reality function." That is, stereotypes are useful tools for dealing with the world. Confronted with a snake or a fawn, our immediate behavior is determined by generalized beliefs—stereotypes—about snakes and fawns. Stereotypes are, in fact, merely one aspect of the mind's ability to make generalizations, without which science and mathematics, not to mention, as the snake/fawn example shows, much of everyday life, would be impossible.

---

## Faulty Assertions

Discussions of racial profiling almost inevitably are based on an assertion that racial and ethnic groups should be subject to procedures in the criminal justice system based on their *representation in the population* rather than by the *number of crimes they commit*. But the justice system is not the House of Representatives. There is no constitutional guarantee of equal representation in the criminal dockets. Blacks are overrepresented for one simple reason—they commit many crimes at multiples above other racial groups. This propensity toward violent crime is probably the nation's number one social problem. Yet liberals, out of either willful naiveté or chutzpah, choose to pretend it doesn't exist. Senator Robert Torricelli, for instance, made this claim at the confirmation hearings of attorney general John Ashcroft: "Statistically, it cannot be borne out that certain ethnic or racial groups disproportionately commit crimes. They do not." It would be interesting to know where he is getting his statistics.

William Tucker, *Weekly Standard*, June 18, 2001.

---

At some level, everybody knows this stuff, even the guardians of the "racial profiling" flame. Jesse Jackson famously, in 1993, confessed that: "There is nothing more

174

painful to me at this stage in my life than to walk down the street and hear footsteps and start thinking about robbery, then look around and see somebody white and feel relieved." Here is Sandra Seegars of the Washington, D.C., Taxicab Commission: "Late at night, if I saw young black men dressed in a slovenly way, I wouldn't pick them up. . . . And during the day, I'd think twice about it."

Pressed to define "slovenly," Ms. Seegars elaborated thus: "A young black guy with his hat on backwards, shirttail hanging down longer than his coat, baggy pants down below his underwear, and unlaced tennis shoes." Now there's a stereotype for you! Ms. Seegars is, of course, black.

Law-enforcement officials are simply employing the same stereotypes as you, me, Jesse, and Sandra, but taking the opposite course of action. What we seek to avoid, they pursue. They do this for reasons of simple efficiency. A policeman who concentrates a disproportionate amount of his limited time and resources on young black men is going to uncover far more crimes—and therefore be far more successful in his career—than one who biases his attention toward, say, middle-aged Asian women. It is, as Chief Parks said, common sense.

Similarly with the tail of the tadpole-racial-profiling issues that do not involve black people. China is known to have obtained a top-secret warhead design. Among those with clearance to work on that design are people from various kinds of national and racial background. Which ones should investigators concentrate on? The Swedes? The answer surely is: They should first check out anyone who has family or friends in China, who has made trips to China, or who has met with Chinese officials. This would include me, for example—my father-in-law is an official of the Chinese Communist Party. Would I then have been "racially profiled"?

## A Decline in Effective Police Work

It is not very surprising to learn that the main fruit of the "racial profiling" hysteria has been a decline in the efficiency of police work. In Philadelphia, a federal court order now requires police to fill out both sides of an 8½-by-11 sheet on every citizen contact. Law-enforcement agencies nationwide are engaged in similar statistics-gathering exercises, under pressure from federal lawmakers like U.S. Rep. John Conyers, who has announced that he will introduce a bill to force police agencies to keep detailed information about traffic stops. ("The struggle goes on," declared Rep. Conyers. The struggle that is going on, it sometimes seems, is a struggle to prevent our police forces from accomplishing any useful work at all.)

The mountain of statistics that is being brought forth by all this panic does not, on the evidence so far, seem likely to shed much light on what is happening. The numbers have a way of leading off into infinite regresses of uncertainty. The city of San Jose, Calif., for example, discovered that, yes, the percentage of blacks being stopped was higher than their representation in the city's population. Ah, but patrol cars were computer-assigned to high-crime districts, which are mainly inhabited by minorities. So that over-representation might actually be an under-representation! But then, minorities have fewer cars. . . .

Notwithstanding the extreme difficulty of finding out what is actually happening, we can at least seek some moral and philosophical grounds on which to take a stand either for or against racial profiling. I am going to take it as a given that most readers of this article will be of a conservative inclination, and shall offer only those arguments likely to appeal to persons so inclined. If you seek arguments of other kinds, they are not hard to find—just pick up your newspaper or turn on your TV.

## In Defense of Profiling

Of arguments against racial profiling, probably the ones most persuasive to a conservative are the ones from libertarianism. Many of the stop-and-search cases that brought this matter into the headlines were part of the so-called war on drugs. The police procedures behind them were ratified by court decisions of the 1980s, themselves mostly responding to the rising tide of illegal narcotics. In *U.S. vs. Montoya De Hernandez* (1985) for example, Chief Justice Rehnquist validated the detention of a suspected "balloon swallowing" drug courier until the material had passed through her system, by noting previous invasions upheld by the Court: "[F]irst class mail may be opened without a warrant on less than probable cause . . . Automotive travellers may be stopped . . . near the border without individualized suspicion *even if the stop is based largely on ethnicity* . . ." (My italics.)

The Chief Justice further noted that these incursions are in response to "the veritable national crisis in law enforcement caused by smuggling of illegal narcotics." Many on the political Right feel that the war on drugs is at best misguided, at worst a moral and constitutional disaster. Yet it is naive to imagine that the "racial profiling" hubbub would go away, or even much diminish, if all state and federal drug laws were repealed tomorrow. Black and Hispanic Americans would still be committing crimes at rates higher than citizens of other races. The differential criminality of various ethnic groups is not only, or even mainly, located in drug crimes. In 1997, for example, blacks, who are 13 percent of the U.S. population, comprised 35 percent of those arrested for embezzlement. (It is not generally appreciated that black Americans commit higher levels not only of "street crime," but also of white-collar crime.)

Even without the drug war, diligent police officers would still, therefore, be correct to regard black and Hispanic citizens—other factors duly considered—as more likely to be breaking the law. The Chinese government would still be trying to recruit spies exclusively from among Chinese-born Americans. (The Chinese Communist Party is, in this respect, the keenest "racial profiler" of all.) The Amadou Diallo case—the police were looking for a rapist—would still have happened.

## Randall Kennedy's Argument

The best non-libertarian argument against racial profiling is the one from equality before the law. This has been most cogently presented by Prof. Randall Kennedy of Harvard. Kennedy concedes most of the points I have made. Yes, he says:

> Statistics abundantly confirm that African Americans—and particularly young black men—commit a dramatically disproportionate share of street crime in the United States.

177

This is a sociological fact, not a figment of the media's (or the police's) racist imagination. In recent years, for example, victims of crime report blacks as the perpetrators in around 25 per cent of the violent crimes suffered, although blacks constitute only about twelve percent of the nation's population.

And yes, says Prof. Kennedy, outlawing racial profiling will reduce the efficiency of police work. Nonetheless, for constitutional and moral reasons we should outlaw the practice. If this places extra burdens on law enforcement, well, "racial equality, like all good things in life, costs something; it does not come for free."

There are two problems with this. The first is that Kennedy has minimized the black-white difference in criminality, and therefore that "cost." I don't know where his 25 percent comes from, or what "recent years" means, but I do know that in Department of Justice figures for 1997, victims report 60 percent of robberies as having been committed by black persons. In that same year, a black American was eight times more likely than a non-black to commit homicide— and "non-black" here includes Hispanics, not broken out separately in these figures. A racial-profiling ban, under which police officers were required to stop and question suspects in precise proportion to their demographic representation (in what? the precinct population? the state population? the national population?), would lead to massive inefficiencies in police work. Which is to say, massive declines in the apprehension of criminals.

The other problem is with the special status that Prof. Kennedy accords to race. Kennedy: "Racial distinctions are and should be different from other lines of social stratification." Thus, if it can be shown, as it surely can, that state troopers stop young people more than old people, relative to young people's numerical representation on the road being patrolled, that is of no consequence. If they stop black people more than white people, on the same criterion, that is of large consequence. This, in spite of the fact that the categories "age" and "race" are both rather fuzzy (define "young") and are both useful predictors of criminality. In spite of the fact, too, that the principle of equality before the law does not, and up to now has never been thought to,

178

guarantee equal outcomes for any law-enforcement process, only that a citizen who has come under reasonable suspicion will be treated fairly.

## An Assault on Common Sense

It is on this special status accorded to race that, I believe, we have gone most seriously astray. I am willing, in fact, to say much more than this: In the matter of race, I think the Anglo-Saxon world has taken leave of its senses. The campaign to ban racial profiling is, as I see it, a part of that large, broad-fronted assault on common sense that our over-educated, over-lawyered society has been enduring for some forty years now, and whose roots are in a fanatical egalitarianism, a grim determination not to face up to the realities of group differences, a theological attachment to the doctrine that the sole and sufficient explanation for all such differences is "racism"—which is to say, the malice and cruelty of white people—and a nursed and petted guilt towards the behavior of our ancestors.

At present, Americans are drifting away from the concept of belonging to a single nation. I do not think this drift will be arrested until we can shed the idea that deference to the sensitivities of racial minorities—however overwrought those sensitivities may be, however over-stimulated by unscrupulous mountebanks, however disconnected from reality—trumps every other consideration, including even the maintenance of social order. To shed that idea, we must confront our national hysteria about race, which causes large numbers of otherwise sane people to believe that the hearts of their fellow citizens are filled with malice towards them. So long as we continue to pander to that poisonous, preposterous belief, we shall only wander off deeper into a wilderness of division, mistrust, and institutionalized rancor—that wilderness, the most freshly painted signpost to which bears the legend RACIAL PROFILING.

179

*"Slavery is responsible for having robbed black people of the economic resources necessary to acquire the cultural tools and institutions of the dominant group."*

# The United States Should Pay Reparations for Slavery

Ronald Walters

In the following viewpoint, Ronald Walters contends that the U.S. government should pay reparations to African Americans for the enslavement of their forebears. Even after legal slavery ended, he points out, southern blacks were often brutalized and forced to work on plantations under slavery conditions well into the twentieth century. Slave labor fostered the development of successful factories and corporations but led to poverty and dangerous social conditions for many blacks, Walters maintains. The government should admit that today's racial economic gap is the result of slavery and compensate African Americans for their ancestors' unpaid labor. Walters is Distinguished Leadership Scholar at the University of Maryland.

As you read, consider the following questions:
1. According to Walters, how did slavery fuel the growth of the textile industry in New England?
2. What two minority groups have received reparations from the U.S. government, according to the author?
3. In Walters's opinion, why should the government take most of the responsibility for compensating blacks for slavery?

From "For Slavery? Let's Resolve the Inequity," by Ronald Walters, *World & I*, April 2000. Copyright © 2000 by *World & I*. Reprinted with permission.

We are in a period of history where morality and ethics are emphasized as the primary ingredients of civil virtue. However, one of the most immoral acts in the development of the United States was the enslavement of Africans, compounded by (1) failure to acknowledge that the grandeur of this country was based, in substantial part, upon the monumental resources made possible by unpaid slave labor, and (2) refusal to make reparations for this crime. Most Americans have rejected the strength of America's slave heritage, and in so doing they devalue its contribution to the country's economic strength.

For example, the factory system emerged as an outgrowth of slavery when in 1790 Samuel Slater, an English immigrant who knew the secrets of English textile machinery, built a cotton-spinning mill at Pawtucket, Rhode Island, for a merchant named Moses Brown. This mill, with 72 spindles, became the first successful American factory. By the end of the War of 1812, hundreds of factories, with an estimated 130,000 spindles, were in operation, and by 1840 the number of spindles reached 2 million. Enslaved Africans in the South picked the cotton that fed these spindles and fueled the growth of the textile industry in New England.

This led to larger and more sophisticated manufacturing institutions known as corporations, until in 1865, at the end of the Civil War, a group of businessmen—including Frances Cabot Lowell, Nathan Appleton, and Patrick Tracy Jackson—formed the Boston Manufacturing Company, which later came to be known as the Boston Associates, in Waltham, Massachusetts. This was the first integrated factory in textiles; in other words, it performed every operation. In 1920 the company shifted operations to Lowell, Massachusetts, and became the Merrick Manufacturing Company, and in the 1920s and '30s it bought companies in Massachusetts and New Hampshire, making the manufacturing corporation an entrenched institution in America.

This failure to acknowledge the contribution of African Americans to the country's development fosters such cynicism and alienation that it prevents full faith in the institutionalized version of the American dream. Moreover, it contributes to the differential perceptions and interpretations of

American life by blacks and whites, such as the O.J. [Simpson] murder verdict, the Los Angeles rebellions after the Rodney King verdict, and other racially charged incidents.

In 1998, we completed a cycle of national discussions on race known as "The Race Initiative," sponsored by President Bill Clinton. However, this project failed to capture the imagination of the American people, partially because of the desperate attempt of conservatives to deny and suppress a discussion of the importance of the slave origins of American wealth and the country's debt to African Americans. Contrast this modern flight from responsibility to the words of William Pitt the Younger, head of state in 1807 when the English Parliament was passing legislation prohibiting the slave trade:

> I therefore congratulate this House, the country and the world that this great point is gained: that we may now consider this trade as having received its condemnation; that its sentence is sealed; that this curse of mankind is seen by the House in its true light; and that the greatest stigma on our national character which ever yet existed is about to be removed. And sir, (which is still more important) that mankind, I trust, in general, are now likely to be delivered from the greatest practical evil that ever has afflicted the human race—from the severest and most extensive calamity recorded in the history of the world!

Pitt did not temporize about the depth of the crime of slavery, as is generally the case in so many quarters today. Thus, when President Clinton, while traveling in Africa in March 1998, used language that appeared to broach an apology for slavery, by admitting that America had not always done the right thing by Africa, members of the Republican Party in Congress rose to denounce him immediately.

## Slavery and Pauperization

The distinguished black American intellectual W.E.B. DuBois noted in his study *The Philadelphia Negro* (1897) that "everywhere slavery was accompanied by pauperization" and that this condition of poverty prevented blacks from establishing a black middle class when wave upon wave of poor migrants from the South overwhelmed the fledgling black elite and defined poverty as the basic condition of the black urban ghetto.

DuBois, Professors Kenneth Clark and William Wilson, and others have established a clear link between the "pauperization" of blacks and such social conditions as high crime rates, poor health, educational gaps, family social disorganization, high unemployment rates, poor neighborhoods, and substandard housing and other structures.

The reasons for these conditions, which characterize the black urban ghetto and the institutions within it even today, have been mystified, but slavery is responsible for having robbed black people of the economic resources necessary to acquire the cultural tools and institutions of the dominant group.

These economic resources would have made possible the construction of schools and colleges that would have long ago closed any cultural gap in test scores and produced a large middle class of blacks that would have developed companies the equal of AT&T, IBM, or Morgan Stanley. This would have institutionalized a private economy that would have provided a substantial foundation for financial independence within the black community. The dimensions of this debt have attracted individuals such as Nobel Prize–winning Yale economist Boris Bittker, who analyzed this problem in his book *The Case for Black Reparations* as early as 1973.

## The Longevity of Slavery

One reason given for denying reparations to African Americans and according them to Asian Americans is that the events that constituted a basis for the latter group occurred more recently, during World War II. However, it is one of the myths of American history and its historians that slavery ended in 1865. In fact, although legal slavery ended, in many places, especially in the South, the practice continued well into the twentieth century.

The National Archives contains files of letters written in the 1920s, '30s, and '40s and sent to the National Association for the Advancement of Colored People (NAACP) by blacks who were still being held in slavery conditions on plantations in the South, still being forced to work without pay or to receive only symbolic wages, and still being brutalized. Then, debt slavery—where the sharecropping system held many former slaves in legal bondage, forcing them to work to pay mythical debts to landowners, was common.

Finally, the prison system was expanded in the South and utilized to administer the convict-lease system, where blacks were convicted on petty or nonexistent crimes and leased out to work for merchants and plantation owners in slavery conditions. These situations were in many cases merely other forms of slavery, often worse than the original kind.

Marlette. © 1989 by Newsday, Inc. Reprinted with permission.

This system carried well into the twentieth century, as records of the Justice Department show. In a 1996 *Washington Post* article titled "Slavery Did Not End With the Civil War: One Man's Odyssey Into a Nation's Secret Shame," Len Cooper cites a newspaper story that described a Justice Department prosecution of the Dial brothers in Sumpter County, Alabama, in 1954 because they had held blacks in involuntary servitude. This means that the civil rights movement was the force that broke the final link to slavery.

The fact that some blacks were held in slavery until after World War II and that cases of lynching also extended to that period refutes any proposition that slavery ended in 1865. This establishes a modern basis for reparations for the descendants of slaves as legitimate as that of any other group.

# Government Responsibility

We also live in an era when there is much public dialogue about "individual responsibility," rather than the responsibility of government. Yet, in this case, there is both a rejection of individual responsibility for slavery—on the basis of longevity, recency of immigration, or other factors—and a reluctance to acknowledge the culpability of the state in administering the past slave status of African Americans. These have combined into the feeling that since neither individual nor government responsibility was possible, the pursuit of such a public policy was "unrealistic" and used ultimately, by both blacks and whites, to successfully evade an American dialogue about this issue.

Real reparations, however, have been given to other groups. Slavery and the extermination of the Native American are the only truly American holocausts, but whereas the Native Americans have been given land and a system of government, however flawed, black Americans have not been compensated for slavery and certainly have not enjoyed benefits beyond those available to other American citizens. And while reparations have been informally refused blacks, Japanese-American internees during World War II received them.

In fact, it is possible to argue that past attempts made to make amelioration for slavery have been dismantled before they could be implemented, or changed to advantage the majority, whether in the case of Reconstruction, civil rights, or even affirmative action.

I refer to the responsibility of government as the main authority figure in arranging recompense for slavery because at every stage individual Americans were permitted to practice slavery by writ of law, by each of the colonial territories even before there was a United States of America, certainly by the Constitutional Congress, and by successive acts of the Supreme Court, the Congress, and the state governments.

There is a deep sensitivity among the descendants of slaves in America today that a substantial part of the social distance between them and white America was created by the process of enslavement. Despite the rampant economic growth, the structural distance in economic resources has been maintained in that blacks still have only one-tenth the wealth, more than twice the poverty rate, and double the unemployment rate of whites.

This means that the failure to replace appropriated black economic resources as an "unrealistic" public policy is one of the powerful factors that results in the inability of both blacks and whites to "get beyond race," because the reluctant pace of resolving the inequality continues to place an emphasis on the fact that blacks in America are the only group expected to come all the way up the rough side of the mountain—in the most economically competitive society in the world—without the requisite resources to do so.

The other factor, of course, is the persistence of racism in nearly every sector of American life, a fact that continues to transfer resources to whites, buttressed by the attempt to attribute the subordinate status of blacks to their lack of effort, or their natural inferiority, as rendered in such works as *The Bell Curve*, by Charles Murray and Richard Herrnstein.

At the height of the attempt to pass civil rights laws in the 1960s, those opposed argued that the key to full black participation in American life is not the passage of laws but social acceptance. The other side of this equation is that acceptance must also come from blacks, and its foundation begins with acknowledging the role of the dominant culture in (1) the crime of slavery, (2) the equal crime of pretending that the gap between Africans and others is a natural condition rather than a product of enslavement, and (3) the need to make material recompense for the unpaid labor of those enslaved.

In the famous picture of George Washington crossing the Delaware River, there is a black man in the boat at the oars. His name was Prince Whipple, the son of a king in West Africa. He was sent to America for education but was instead enslaved by William Whipple, one of the signatories to the Declaration of Independence. Whipple seconded Prince to be Washington's aide when Whipple went to war.

As Whipple was leaving to join the fight for American independence as an officer, Prince Whipple was recorded to have said: "You are going to fight for your liberty, but I have none to fight for." Resolving the debt of slavery through reparations will help to combine what has been two different historical struggles for "freedom" into one.

*"Reparations [for slavery] would be a gross injustice, punishing innocent people for a crime they did not commit."*

# The United States Should Not Pay Reparations for Slavery

Robert Tracinski

The United States does not owe reparations to the current descendants of African American slaves, argues Robert Tracinski in the following viewpoint. Today's blacks did not experience slavery and cannot make any provable claim that the bondage of their ancestors negatively affects their lives. Moreover, Tracinski points out, most nonblack Americans are descended from families that did not own slaves or from families that immigrated to the country after the end of slavery. Even the descendants of slave owners cannot be held accountable for the actions of their forebears, the author states. Requiring the federal government or individual corporations to compensate blacks for slavery would only increase racial tensions, he concludes. Tracinski is editor of *The Intellectual Activist*, a monthly journal.

As you read, consider the following questions:
1. In Tracinski's opinion, what is the premise behind all forms of racism?
2. What is the real cause of black unemployment, crime, and poverty, in the author's view?
3. According to Tracinski, in what way has the United States already "paid" for slavery?

O ver the past few years, a movement composed of liability lawyers and self-titled "civil rights activists" has been trying to revive a deservedly obscure idea: the payment of reparations for the injustices committed under slavery. These activists are undeterred by the fact that none of the original victims or villains of slavery are still alive. Reparations, they say, should be paid by the US government and some long-lived corporations, to compensate the current-day descendants of slaves for the wrongs done to their ancestors.

The most prominent step toward reparations is the formation, late [in the year 2000], of the Reparations Assessment Group, a consortium of academics and liability lawyers led by Harvard Law School Professor Charles Ogletree. The group was formed to prepare civil lawsuits against the federal government and some corporations, ostensibly on behalf of the descendants of slaves.

The case for such reparations is two-fold. First, reparations activists claim that compensation to the descendants of slaves is just, because today's blacks are the "victims" of slavery, and "the victims of unjust enrichment should be compensated." Second, they claim that reparations would help "bridge the racial divide" in America and "heal the wounds of slavery."

In reality, reparations would be a gross injustice, punishing innocent people for a crime they did not commit. Even worse, the campaign for reparations will not "heal the wounds of slavery" but will perpetuate racial conflict.

## Basic Principles of Justice

In order to understand why the campaign for reparations is unjust, we have to look, not just at legal precedent, but at the basic moral principles at the foundation of American law.

One of those principles is the idea that justice is *individual*, not racial. Human beings exist as individuals, with each person responsible for his own choices and actions and entitled to be judged on his own character, not on the color of his skin. By contrast, racism consists of treating a person, not as a self-responsible individual, but as an interchangeable cog of some larger racial collective.

If this racist view is implemented in law, the result is man-

188

ifestly unjust. Suppose, for example, that a bank robber has just made his getaway, and the police are in hot pursuit. All they know about the criminal is that witnesses say he was black. So they round up the first black man they find, haul him off to jail, give him a summary trial, and send him to prison for life. He protests that he is not the person who robbed the bank, but his tormenters say: "Who cares? We know that this crime was committed by a black person, and we punished a black person. It doesn't matter which one."

If this example does not sound entirely fictional, it certainly is not. This was the racist approach behind lynchings in the Old South.

The premise behind every form of racism, we must bear in mind, is the rejection of the principle that justice is individual. As the novelist and philosopher Ayn Rand observed, "Racism is the lowest, most crudely primitive form of collectivism. . . . [It] means, in practice, that a man is to be judged, not by his own character and actions, but by the characters and actions of a collective of ancestors." The racist approach consists of declaring that an individual's own thoughts and choices are irrelevant; all that matters, to the racist, is a person's membership in a racial group.

Racism, as a philosophical and legal issue, comes down to one basic question: Is justice collective, i.e., should a person be judged by his race—or is justice individual, i.e., should a person be judged on his own merits.

By this standard, how do reparations for slavery measure up?

## Reparations and Tort Laws

Let us examine the attempt to seek reparations through the tort laws. The purpose of tort law is to provide compensation to persons who have been unjustly harmed, to be paid by those persons who are responsible for the harm. To have a legitimate case for reparations, one must first identify an individual who has been directly, provably harmed—and then one must identify an individual who is directly, provably responsible for that harm.

Yet that is precisely what *cannot* be done in this case. Every individual slave and every individual slaveholder is long dead. There is no person living who can be a party to a lawsuit seeking reparations for slavery—*and* there is no individual still alive who can be brought before the court and named as the defendant.

This, incidentally, is a crucial difference between reparations for slavery and reparations for Japanese-Americans who were interned during World War II, or Jews whose assets were stolen during the Holocaust. In both of those cases, victims of the injustice were still alive and able to seek compensation, although in some cases compensation for stolen wealth was also awarded to the direct, first-generation descendants of victims who had died.

The case of slavery, however, is fundamentally different. It is an attempt to extend liability, not merely one generation, but through multiple generations, into the *indefinite* past.

## Today's Blacks Did Not Experience Bondage

The absurdity of this attempt is captured in a single sentence from a news report on this issue, which describes "a growing number of slave descendants who are calling for the US government to repay them for 246 years of bondage." The absurdity is that these people cannot be "re-paid" for 246 years of bondage, because they did not experience that bondage. The people who are demanding reparations have never been slaves. Moreover, their parents were not slaves, and, except in a few extraordinary cases, their grandparents were not slaves. In a normal case, we have to look back at least *four to five generations* to find ancestors who were actually slaves.

So those who are alive today, who are seeking reparations for slavery, are not in any way the direct victims of slavery. Their connection to the people who actually were slaves is long and remote, traced through more than a century of parents and grandparents who were free to make their own choices, guide their own actions, and pursue their own fortunes. This intervening history makes it impossible to determine objectively the degree or even the existence of slavery's effect on current-day descendants of slaves.

As a parallel example, consider the tens of millions of Americans who are descended from immigrants who came to the country about a century ago. Many of these immigrants came to America with no money, no education, no specialized skills, and no knowledge of the English language. Many, such as Eastern European Jews, had been victims of persecution in their native lands. Yet most of these immigrants worked to pull themselves out of poverty, their children were able to rise into the middle class, their grandchildren attended college—and today, we do not talk about the "lingering legacy of immigration," nor do descendants of immigrants seek reparations for the past persecution of their ancestors. After three or four generations, it is clear that the choices and actions of individuals have had a far greater impact on their well-being than the past condition of their ancestors.

It is important to recognize that the history of blacks in America is not fundamentally different. In the century after slavery—despite legal segregation and the continued influence of racism—black Americans improved their own condition by every measure. Labor force participation rates for blacks were usually higher than for whites, and as a result black poverty rates dropped consistently over the entire century. Other economic and cultural ills were largely absent within a few decades after slavery's end: Black crime rates were no higher than for other groups, and illegitimacy rates were well below 20%. The work and effort of former slaves and their immediate descendants in the century after 1865 largely overcame the injuries suffered by their ancestors.

## Absurd Claims

Incidentally, this gives the lie to the claim that poverty, unemployment, crime, and illegitimacy are the "legacy of slavery." Every one of these ills became epidemic only *after 1960*. It was after the creation of the "Great Society" welfare programs, with their perverse incentives against work and marriage, and the passage of the Civil Rights Act of 1964, which laid the legal foundation for racial preferences, that black crime and illegitimacy rates soared, labor force participation dropped, and poverty rates froze. It is significant that reparations advocates, almost without exception, seek to *expand* the welfare state. In blaming slavery for every problem faced by black Americans, they are trying to divert attention from the disastrous legacy of welfare and "affirmative action."

This history shows the absurdity of the claim that people living today are entitled to compensation for injuries suffered by their ancestors in the indefinite past. Instead, it shows that individuals are capable of taking responsibility for improving their own lives—and indeed, that they fail to progress only when they are convinced *not* to accept that responsibility.

## Who Should Be Punished for Slavery?

So much for the plaintiff's side of the equation. What about the defendant? Is there anyone alive today who may legitimately be punished for the injustices of slavery? How, for example, can a white American today be fined for an injustice that might have been committed by his great-great-grandfather?

The problem is compounded by the fact that the majority of Americans do not descend from slaveholders; their ancestors were either from the non-slave-holding North, or they were immigrants who came to America after the end of slavery. But even if we can find someone of pure slaveholding stock, as it were, someone whose ancestors were all guilty of the crime of slavery—how can we hold that person, today, responsible for actions taken more than a century ago by his forebears? To do so, we would have to judge this person—to quote Ayn Rand, "not by his own character and actions, but by the characters and actions of a collective of ancestors." Yet that is the very essence of racism.

Reparations advocates have offered no answer—literally none—to this argument. The response of Representative John Conyers, who has been promoting reparations in Congress, is typical: "This is not a blame game. We are not looking for who did it or how evil were their motives. Payment is not going to come from who did it. The government assumes responsibility." In other words, Conyers attempts to evade the issue by pretending that "the government"—and not the individuals who pay taxes—will foot the bill.

In that spirit, the proposed reparations suits would target two kinds of legal entities that *are* still "alive" from the days of slavery: the government and those corporations that have been in continuous existence since before 1865. Remember that reparations advocates still have not identified someone with standing to sue, so there is still no proper plaintiff. But they argue that we do have a defendant, that the federal government and private corporations can be held culpable for the evils of slavery.

Let us consider the federal government first.

Seeking compensation from the United States government evades the fact that the federal government has already paid an enormous cost to *end* slavery by fighting the Civil War. Even if we do not count the cost in human lives, which was enormous, we can at least count the cost in dollars. The Civil War cost the US government about $15 billion—an astronomical sum in 1865, equivalent to hundreds of billions of dollars today. Adding 135 years of compound interest—a typical technique used to calculate demands for reparations—the federal government's cost rises to trillions of dollars in current value.

---

## Opposition to Reparations

Many black voices have risen in opposition to the very idea of reparations for slavery. Walter Williams, chairman of the Department of Economics at George Mason University, describes the call for reparations as "just another scam" and argues that at this point in history, "slave owners cannot be punished and slaves cannot be rewarded. Black people in our country have gone further than any other race of people. You cannot portray blacks as victims. It's an insult to their progress and success. Most of [today's] problems have nothing to do with race; they're social and economic."

The call for reparations, states Michael Meyer, executive director of the New York Civil Rights Coalition, "is an embarrassment of muddled thinking—but then, foolishness and pie-in-the-sky sounding off are par for those who believe the world owes them. . . . However one defines it, 'reparations' is just another word for the old racial hustle."

Jay Parker, *World & I*, April 2000.

---

More fundamentally, however, the federal government has no funds of its own, no cache of savings left over from, say, taxes on cotton. All of the government's money is extracted from today's taxpayers. The government is merely a middleman who would pass the cost for reparations on to the taxpayers. That leaves us where we began: the manifest injustice of punishing people for the crimes committed by some of their distant ancestors.

## Lawsuits Against Corporations?

Now let us turn to the second proposed defendant: corporations.

The proposed reparations suits would target a few long-lived corporations which at one time used slave labor or profited indirectly from slavery. On this basis, the proposed suits would lay claim to some significant portion of the current assets of these corporations. Early [in 2001], for example, the state of California passed a law requiring every insurance company that does business in California—which includes every major American insurance company—to disclose whether it once offered "slave insurance," insurance offered to protect slave-owners against financial losses from the death or escape of a slave. The law was clearly designed to aid in building a reparations case against these corporations.

Such lawsuits, however, face a fundamental barrier: How would one prove that the current assets or profits of a corporation are caused by profits made more than 135 years ago under slavery? Consider the following example.

The first major insurance company to comply with the California law was Aetna, which has been in existence since the 1840s. A search of Aetna's records revealed a total of *five* slave insurance policies. That is a minuscule amount for a major insurance company. But also reflect on what has happened since. Aetna, for example, was reorganized in the late 1860s, radically changed its practices to weather a series of economic depressions in the 1870s, and went on to survive through wars, through the Great Depression, and through every economic event that has occurred since.

It is obvious that after 135 years of ups and downs, during which time fortunes have risen and fallen, thousands of new companies have been formed, thousands of old ones have gone out of existence, and the nation's economy has been radically transformed twice, first by heavy industry, then by information technology—after all of this time, any profits once gained from slavery have been rendered irrelevant.

A tort claim that attempts to trace a portion of a company's profits from 135 years ago to its assets today is arbitrary and unreasonable. It is like the claim that the flapping of a butterfly's wings in the Amazon causes a hurricane in the Northern Atlantic. It is, in principle, unprovable.

More fundamentally, any such unlimited liability subjects the current stockholders of a company to the arbitrary and unpredictable expropriation of their wealth. If the current owners of an asset may be punished without limit for the wrongs committed by its past owners, then no one could ever hold clear title to a single piece of property or share of stock. . . .

## Racial Collectivism

From an individualist perspective, there is neither a proper plaintiff nor a proper defendant in this suit. To reparations advocates, however, these parties are easy to identify—so long as one agrees to abandon individual justice and herd mankind into racial collectives. From this perspective of racial collectivism, the plaintiff in this case is "black America," which is seeking compensation from the defendant, "white America."

Some reparations advocates openly acknowledge this collectivist approach. Tulane University Professor Robert Westley notes that the demand for reparations is the result of a "sea-change . . . regarding the proper evaluation of the antiracist agenda set by the Civil Rights Movement" which "relied on the rhetoric of equality rights." Westley goes on to say—correctly—that this "liberal legal framework" and its notion of equal rights is the primary barrier to reparations—which he says must be overcome. In a truly Orwellian climax, he quotes the work of Professor Thomas Pettigrew, who defines "the new racism" to include "individualistic conceptions of how opportunity and social stratification operate in American society." In other words, individualism is racism. Westley attempts to wipe out the concept of individual justice, establishing racial collectivism as the only basis for morality and law.

This gives the lie to the claim that reparations will "heal the wounds" of slavery and racism. Reparations would do the opposite: they would promote a collectivist, racial concept of justice. The philosophical perspective behind reparations encourages men to look on their fellows, not as individuals with their own independent characters and merits, but only as members of some competing, antagonistic racial collective.

Rather than healing historical wounds, this is an approach that is guaranteed to keep those wounds open forever.

*"All America loses when any person is denied or forced out of a job because of sexual orientation."*

# Congress Should Ban Antigay Job Discrimination

Bill Clinton

In the following viewpoint, Bill Clinton argues in favor of the passage of legislation that would prohibit job discrimination on the basis of sexual orientation. Clinton maintains that enacting such a law would be a civil rights victory akin to the passage of laws banning employment discrimination on the basis of race, gender, religion, or disability. He also contends that discrimination will decrease as more Americans learn that they have gay friends, relatives, and coworkers. Clinton was the forty-second president of the United States. This viewpoint is excerpted from his keynote address to the Human Rights Campaign dinner in Washington, D.C., on October 8, 1997.

As you read, consider the following questions:
1. According to Clinton, how did President Harry Truman help define the civil rights struggle?
2. How does the author describe the "American Dream"?
3. What does Clinton mean when he says "we have to broaden the imagination of America"?

From "Keynote Address," by Bill Clinton, SIECUS Report, April/May 1998.

I want this to be a country where every child and every person who is responsible enough to work for it can live the American Dream. I want this country to embrace the wider world and continue to be the strongest force for peace and freedom and prosperity, and I want us to come together across all our lines of difference into one America.

That is my vision. It drives me every day. I think if we really could create a society where there is opportunity for all and responsibility from all and we believed in a community of all Americans, we could truly meet every problem we have and seize every opportunity we have.

For more than two centuries now, our country has had to meet challenge after challenge after challenge. We have had to continue to lift ourselves beyond what we thought America meant. Our ideals were never meant to be frozen in stone or time. Keep in mind, when we started out with Thomas Jefferson's credo that all of us are created equal by God, what that really meant in civic political terms was that you had to be white, you had to be male, and that wasn't enough—you had to own property, which would have left my crowd out when I was a boy.

Over time, we have had to redefine the words that we started with, not because there was anything wrong with them and their universal power and strength of liberty and justice, but because we were limited in our imaginations about how we could live and what we were capable of and how we should live. Indeed, the story of how we kept going higher and higher and higher to new and higher definitions—of equality and dignity and freedom is in its essence the fundamental story of our country.

## All Americans Means All Americans

[More than] fifty years ago, President Truman stood at a new frontier in our defining struggle on civil rights. Slavery had ended a long time before, but segregation remained. Harry Truman stood before the Lincoln Memorial and said, "It is more important today than ever to ensure that all Americans enjoy the rights [of freedom and equality]. When I say all Americans, I mean all Americans."

Well, my friends, all Americans still means all Americans.

We all know that it is an ideal and not perfectly real now. We all know that some of the old kinds of discrimination we have sought to rid ourselves of by law and purge our spirits of still exist in America today. We all know that there is continuing discrimination against gays and lesbians. But we also know that if we're ever going to build one America, then all Americans—including you and those whom you represent—have got to be part of it.

To be sure, no President can grant rights. Our ideals and our history hold that they are inalienable, embedded in our Constitution, amplified over time by our courts and legislature. I cannot grant them—but I am bound by my oath of office and the burden of history to reaffirm them.

All America loses if we let prejudice and discrimination stifle the hopes or deny the potential of a single American. All America loses when any person is denied or forced out of a job because of sexual orientation. Being gay, the last time I thought about it, seemed to have nothing to do with the ability to read a balance book, fix a broken bone, or change a spark plug.

## A Fundamental Concept

For generations, the American Dream has represented a fundamental compact among our people. If you take responsibility and work hard, you have the right to achieve a better life for yourself and a better future for your family. Equal opportunity for all, special privileges for none—a fate shared by Americans regardless of political views. We believe—or we all *say* we believe—that all citizens should have the chance to rise as far as their God-given talents will take them. What counts is energy and honesty and talent. No arbitrary distinctions should bar the way.

So when we deny opportunity because of ancestry or religion, race or gender, disability or sexual orientation, we break the compact. It is wrong. And it should be illegal. Once again, I call upon Congress to honor our most cherished principles and make the Employment Non-Discrimination Act the law of the land. [This act was first proposed in Congress during the early 1990s, but had not been passed into law as of 2001.]

199

I also come here tonight to ask you for another favor. Protecting the civil rights of all Americans. Let me say, I thank you very much for your support of my nominee for the Office of Civil Rights, Bill Lee. I thank you for that. But he, too, comes from a family that has known discrimination and now he is being discriminated against, not because there is anything wrong with his qualifications, not because anybody believes he is not even-tempered, but because some members of the Senate disagree with his views on affirmative action.

## Heterosexism in the Workplace

Heterosexism creates havoc in the workplace because it sends out the message that all employees should be heterosexual. For those readers who are heterosexual, imagine for a moment that you are gay and that I am your heterosexual office mate. If I assume that you are like me—heterosexual—I make it difficult for you to tell me that I am wrong. If it is difficult for you to tell me, you will keep your mouth shut and I will continue to assume. I will do things and say things that are inappropriate and sometimes offensive and you won't trust me. Because you have a secret you assume I don't want to hear, you don't feel comfortable with me and don't collaborate as much as you might. That makes it difficult for you to be fully productive and reduces the effectiveness of our teamwork.

As a manager, if I assume that everyone who works for me is a heterosexual person, I am less likely to be concerned about gay issues in the workplace; I am less aware of the toll of inappropriate comments on homosexuality; I am less inclined to think it worth the company's while to educate employees about gay and lesbian issues; I am less likely to use inclusive language; I am also less likely to hear from gay, lesbian, or bisexual employees about the difficulties they face in doing their job. That clearly would make me a less effective manager.

Brian McNaught, *Gay Issues in the Workplace*, 1993.

Now, if I have to appoint a head of the Office of Civil Rights who is against affirmative action, it's going to be vacant a long time. That office is not there primarily to advocate or promote the policies of the government when it comes to affirmative action. It is there to enforce the existing laws against discrimination. You hope someday you will have one of those existing laws. We need somebody to enforce the laws, and Bill Lee should be confirmed, and I ask you to help me to get him confirmed.

## Broadening the Imagination of America

I'd just like to say one more word. There are some people who aren't in this room tonight who aren't comfortable yet with you and won't be comfortable with me for being here. On issue after issue involving gays and lesbians, survey after survey shows that the most important determinant of people's attitudes is whether they are aware—whether they knowingly have had a family or a friendship or a work relation with a gay person.

Now, I hope that we will embrace good people who are trying to overcome their fears. After all, all of us can look back in history and see what the right thing to do was. It is quite another thing to look ahead and light the way. Most people are preoccupied with the burdens of daily living. Most of us, as we grow older, become—whether we like it or not—somewhat more limited in our imaginations. So I think one of the greatest things we have to do still is just to increase the ability of Americans who do not yet know that gays and lesbians are their fellow Americans in every sense of the word to feel that way. I think it's very important.

When I say, "I believe all Americans means all Americans," I see the faces of the friends of 35 years. When I say, "all Americans means all Americans," I see the faces of the people who stood up when I asked the people who are part of our Administration to stand tonight. When I say, "all Americans means all Americans," I see kind, unbelievably generous, giving people back in my home state who helped my family and my friends when they were in need. It is a different story when you know what you are seeing.

So I say to you tonight, should we change the law? You bet. Should we keep fighting discrimination? Absolutely. Is this Hate Crimes Conference important? It is *terribly* important. But we have to broaden the imagination of America. We are redefining, in practical terms, the immutable ideals that have guided us from the beginning. Again I say, we have to make sure that for every single person in our country, all Americans means all Americans.

After experiencing the horrors of the Civil War and witnessing the transformation of the previous century, Walt Whitman said that our greatest strength was that we are an embracing nation. In his words, a "Union, holding all, fusing, absorbing, tolerating all." Let us move forward in the spirit of that one America. Let us realize that this is a good obligation that has been imposed upon our generation, and a grand opportunity once again to lift America to a higher level of unity, once again to redefine and to strengthen and to ensure one America for a new century and a new generation of our precious children. Thank you and God bless you.

8

*"The truth is, most gay people are not
victims, at least not in the economic sense.
. . . Despite intense psychological, social,
and cultural hostility, we have managed to
fare pretty well economically."*

# Laws Banning Antigay Job Discrimination Are Unnecessary

Andrew Sullivan

Gays and lesbians do not need special laws protecting them from employment discrimination, argues Andrew Sullivan in the following viewpoint. In his opinion, homosexuals have not been systematically denied employment in the same way that minorities and women have. Although cases of antigay job discrimination do occur, they have not kept homosexuals from achieving economic success, states Sullivan. Rather than fighting for measures prohibiting antigay employment discrimination, gays and lesbians should focus on genuine equal-rights battles, such as the struggle for gay marriage and the inclusion of gays in the military. Sullivan, a senior editor of the weekly magazine the *New Republic*, is the author of *Virtually Normal: An Argument About Homosexuality*.

As you read, consider the following questions:
1. In Sullivan's opinion, what is the "germ of truth" in the argument that antigay discrimination laws amount to special rights?
2. What has kept gays and lesbians from becoming economic victims, in the author's view?

B efore I make myself irreparably unpopular, I might as well
start with a concession. Almost all the arguments the fundamentalist right uses against gay "special rights" are phony
ones. If there's legal protection for blacks, whites, Jews, Latinos, women, the disabled, and now men in the workplace,
then it's hard to see why homosexuals should be excluded.

It's also true that such laws would ban discrimination
against straights as well as gays, and so they target no single
group for "special" protection. Nevertheless, there's a reason the special rights rhetoric works, and that is because it
contains a germ of truth. However evenhanded antidiscrimination laws are in principle, in practice they're designed to
protect the oppressed. So while the laws pretend to ban discrimination on the neutral grounds of sex, race, ethnicity, or
disability, they really exist to protect women, blacks, Latinos, the disabled, and so on. They are laws that create a
class of victims and a battery of lawyers and lobbyists to
protect them.

## A Whiny Push for Rights

The real question, then, is this: Are gay people generally victims in employment? Have we historically been systematically barred from jobs in the same way that, say, women,
blacks, and the disabled have? And is a remedy therefore
necessary? My own view is that, while there are some particular cases of discrimination against homosexuals, for the
most part getting and keeping jobs is hardly the most pressing issue we face. Aided by our talents, by the ability of each
generation to avoid handing on poverty to the next, and by
the two-edged weapon of the closet, we have, by and large,
avoided becoming economic victims. Even in those states
where job-protection laws have been enacted, sexual orientation cases have made up a minuscule proportion of the
whole caseload.

Most people—gay and straight—know this to be true; and
so they sense that the push for gay employment rights is un-
convincing and whiny. I think they're right. The truth is,
most gay people are not victims, at least not in the economic
sense. We may not be much richer than most Americans, but
there's little evidence that we are much poorer. Despite in-

tense psychological, social, and cultural hostility, we have managed to fare pretty well economically in the past few generations. Instead of continually whining that we need job protection, we should be touting our economic achievements, defending the free market that makes them possible, investing our resources in our churches and charities and social institutions, and politically focusing on the areas where we clearly are discriminated against by our own government.

---

## A Right Worth Fighting For

Same-sex marriage would not force anyone to honor or approve of gay or lesbian relationships against their will. But it would enable those of us who are involved in gay or lesbian relationships to get the rest of society to understand that we take these relationships just as seriously as heterosexual married couples take theirs. And without marriage, we remain second-class citizens—excluded, for no good reason, from participating in one of the basic institutions of society.

Ralph Wedgewood, *Harvard Gay and Lesbian Review*, Fall 1997.

---

The problems of gay and lesbian Americans are not, after all, systematic exclusion from employment. They are (to name a few off the top of my head): a recourse to the closet, a lack of self-esteem, an inability to form lasting relationships, the threat of another epidemic, exclusion from our own churches, and our own government's denial of basic rights, such as marriage, immigration, and military service. In this sense, employment discrimination is a red herring. National gay rights groups love it because they are part of the lobbyist-lawyer nexus that will gain from it and because their polls tell them it's the least objectionable of our aims. But anyone could tell them it's the least objectionable because it's the least relevant.

## Victim-Mongering

Of course, we're told that until we're protected from discrimination in employment, we'll never be able to come out of the closet and effect the deeper changes we all want. But this is more victim-mongering. Who says gay people can't risk something for their own integrity? Who says a civil rights revolution can only occur when every single protection is already in place? If African-Americans in the 1960s had waited for such a moment, there would still be segregation in Alabama.

Our national leaders should spend less time making excuses for us and more time challenging us to risk our own lives and, yes, if necessary, jobs to come out and make a difference for the next generation. An "equal rights" rather than "special rights" agenda would focus on those areas in which gay people really are discriminated against. After all, have you heard any fundamentalist "special rights" rhetoric in the marriage debate? Or in the military battle? Not a squeak. What you hear instead is a revealing mumble of bigotry in opposition. And in these areas of clear government discrimination, we stand on firm, moral ground instead of the muddy bog of interest-group politics. In an equal-rights politics, we reverse the self-defeating logic of victim culture. We are proud and proactive instead of defensive and cowed. And we stop framing a movement around the tired 1970s mantra of "what we want" and start building one around the 1990s vision of "who we actually want to be."

# Periodical Bibliography

The following articles have been selected to supplement the diverse views presented in this chapter.

| | |
|---|---|
| Elizabeth Birch | "Earth to Andrew," *Advocate*, May 26, 1998. |
| Ida L. Castro | "Worth More than We Earn," *National Forum: The Phi Kappa Phi Journal*, Spring 1997. |
| Sanford Cloud Jr. | "A National Dialogue on Race Can Be More than Mere Talk," *Christian Science Monitor*, March 5, 1998. |
| Julia Duin | "Self-Defense Often Best Against Sex Harassment," *Insight*, February 7, 2000. |
| John Fonte | "The Inclusion Illusion," *American Outlook*, Summer 1999. |
| George Fraser | "The Slight Edge: Valuing and Managing Diversity," *Vital Speeches*, February 1, 1998. |
| Maggie Gallagher | "Are You a Bigot?" *Conservative Chronicle*, April 19, 2000. |
| Alan Jenkins | "See No Evil," *Nation*, June 28, 1999. |
| Maureen Kelly | "View from the Field," *SIECUS Report*, April/May 1998. |
| George Lipsitz | "Like Crabs in a Barrel: Why Interethnic Antiracism Matters Now," *Colorlines*, Winter 1999. |
| David B. Mixner | "Knowing When (Not) to Compromise," *Gay and Lesbian Review*, Summer 2000. |
| Jay Parker | "Reparations for Slavery? Don't Perpetuate Division," *World & I*, April 2000. |
| William Tucker | "The Tragedy of Racial Profiling," *Weekly Standard*, June 18, 2001. |
| Chas Walker | "Race, Reparations, and Freedom of the Press," *Political Affairs*, June 2001. |
| Naomi Wolf | "Who's Sorry Now?" *George*, August 1998. |
| Anne Wortham | "Martin Luther King's Flawed Dream," *World & I*, June 1998. |

# For Further Discussion

## Chapter 1

1. Richard Morin and Michael H. Cottman use survey research and anecdotal examples to support their claim that racial discrimination is commonplace. Dinesh D'Souza uses statistics and analogies to buttress his argument that some forms of racial discrimination are justified. Ward Connerly relies mainly on personal experience to back his contention that racial discrimination has diminished. Which type of argument do you find more compelling? Why?

2. Diana Furchtgott-Roth argues that women no longer encounter significant wage discrimination, while Ellen Bravo contends that women continue to earn less than men even when they have the same level of seniority and experience as their male counterparts. Both authors incorporate statistical data to back up their conclusions. In your opinion, which author's use of statistics is more effective? Explain.

3. Harriet Schwartz argues that gays and lesbians face significant discrimination in the workplace, while Concerned Women for America (CWA) contends that homosexuals have not exhibited an inability to obtain income or status because of their sexual preference. Schwartz is a writer for a weekly magazine focusing on gay and lesbian issues, while CWA is a religious conservative advocacy organization. Does knowing this information about Schwartz and CWA influence your assessment of their arguments? Why or why not?

## Chapter 2

1. The editors of the *New Criterion* argue that affirmative action discriminates against whites by requiring the preferential treatment of minorities in hiring and in college admissions. William Raspberry and Derrick Z. Jackson disagree, maintaining that critics of affirmative action fail to recognize the pervasive discrimination that minorities face and are blind to the inherent privileges granted to whites. What evidence do these authors present to support their conclusions? Which of these arguments is more persuasive? Why?

2. How would Rebecca T. Alpert respond to Paul Craig Roberts's contention that reverse discrimination occurs in "politically correct" educational programs that depict whites as evil and oppressive? Explain your answer, using examples from the viewpoints.

3. Andrew Sullivan contends that antiwhite racism on the part of minorities is rarely condemned. Leny Mendoza Strobel maintains that the complexities of white privilege are rarely identified and addressed. How do the arguments of these two authors reflect differing views on the nature of racism? Explain.

## Chapter 3

1. Robert C. Scott argues that affirmative action policies help to counteract the lingering effects of discrimination on women and minorities. Roger Clegg contends that affirmative action causes discrimination by creating unfair hiring preferences for women and nonwhites. Which author do you agree with, and why?

2. Chang-Lin Tien maintains that the use of affirmative action in college admissions benefits all students because it promotes racial diversity on campuses. How does Jason L. Riley respond to the claim that racial diversity enhances academic achievement? Does Riley's argument effectively refute Tien's claims? Why or why not?

## Chapter 4

1. Gene Callahan and William Anderson argue that racial profiling—the use of race as a factor in identifying potential suspects—is a form of discrimination that alienates law-abiding minorities. John Derbyshire contends that racial profiling makes sense because relatively high percentages of blacks and Hispanics commit crimes. In your opinion, is racial profiling justified as a means of reducing criminal activity? Why or why not? Use evidence from the viewpoints in explaining your answer.

2. Ronald Walters maintains that the U.S. government should pay economic reparations to African Americans for the enslavement of their ancestors. Robert Tracinski disagrees, arguing that the descendants of slave owners are not responsible for the actions of their forebears and that reparations would increase rather than decrease racial tensions. In each viewpoint, try to find two supporting arguments that you personally agree with. Why do you agree with them?

3. The viewpoints in this chapter include several recommendations for counteracting institutional discrimination. Consider each recommendation and then list arguments for and against each one. Note whether the arguments are based on facts, values, emotions, or other considerations. If you believe a recommendation should not be considered at all, explain why.

# Organizations to Contact

The editors have compiled the following list of organizations concerned with the issues debated in this book. The descriptions are derived from materials provided by the organizations. All have publications or information available for interested readers. The list was compiled on the date of publication of the present volume; the information provided here may change. Be aware that many organizations take several weeks or longer to respond to inquiries, so allow as much time as possible.

**American Civil Liberties Union (ACLU)**
125 Broad St., 18th Fl., New York, NY 10004
(212) 549-2500 • fax: (212) 549-2646
website: www.aclu.org
The ACLU champions the human rights set forth in the U.S. Constitution. It works to protect the rights of all Americans and to promote equality for women, minorities, and the poor. The organization publishes a variety of handbooks, pamphlets, reports, and newsletters, including the quarterly *Civil Liberties* and the monthly *Civil Liberties Alert*.

**American Immigration Control Foundation (AICF)**
PO Box 525
Monterey, VA 24465
(703) 468-2022 • fax: (703) 468-2024
The AICF is a research and educational organization whose primary goal is to promote a reasonable immigration policy based on national interests and needs. The foundation educates the public on what its members believe are the disastrous effects of uncontrolled immigration. It publishes the monthly newsletter *Border Watch*, as well as several monographs and books on the historical, legal, and demographic aspects of immigration.

**Cato Institute**
1000 Massachusetts Ave. NW, Washington, DC 20001-5403
(202) 842-0200 • fax: (202) 842-3490
e-mail: cato@cato.org • website: www.cato.org
The Cato Institute is a libertarian public policy research foundation dedicated to limiting the role of government and protecting individual liberties. It researches claims of discrimination and opposes affirmative action. The institute offers numerous publications, including the *Cato Journal*, the bimonthly newsletter *Cato Policy Report*, and the quarterly magazine *Regulation*.

## Center for the Study of White American Culture
245 W. 4th Ave., Roselle, NJ 07203
(908) 241-5439
e-mail: contact@euroamerican.org
website: www.euroamerican.org

The center is a multiracial organization that supports cultural exploration and self-discovery among white Americans. It also encourages dialogue among all racial and cultural groups concerning the role of white American culture in the larger American society. It publishes the Whiteness Papers series, including "Decentering Whiteness" and "White Men and the Denial of Racism."

## Center for Women Policy Studies (CWPS)
1211 Connecticut Ave. NW, Suite 312, Washington, DC 20036
(202) 872-1770 • fax: (202) 296-8962
e-mail: cwpsx@aol.com • website: www.centerwomenpolicy.org

CWPS is an independent feminist policy research and advocacy institution established in 1972. The center's programs combine advocacy, research, policy development, and public education to advance the agenda for women's equality and empowerment. CWPS programs address educational equity, family and workplace equality, violence against women, and women's health issues. The center publishes reports, articles, papers, and books such as *The SAT Gender Gap* and *Violence Against Women as a Bias-Motivated Hate Crime*.

## Citizens' Commission on Civil Rights (CCCR)
2000 M St. NW, Suite 400, Washington, DC 20036
(202) 659-5565 • fax: (202) 223-5302
e-mail: citizens@cccr.org • website: www.cccr.org

CCCR monitors the federal government's enforcement of antidiscrimination laws and promotes equal opportunity for all. It publishes reports on affirmative action and desegregation as well as the book *One Nation Indivisible: The Civil Rights Challenge for the 1990s*.

## Commission for Racial Justice (CRJ)
700 Prospect Ave., Cleveland, OH 44115-1110
(216) 736-2100 • fax: (216) 736-2171

CRJ was formed in 1963 by the United Church of Christ in response to racial tensions gripping the nation at that time. Its goal is a peaceful, dignified society where all men and women are equal. CRJ publishes various documents and books, such as *Racism and the Pursuit of Racial Justice* and *A National Symposium on Race and Housing in the United States: Challenges for the 21st Century*.

**Concerned Women for America (CWA)**
1015 15th St. NW, Suite 1100, Washington, DC 20005
(202) 488-7000 • fax: (202) 488-0806
website: www.cwfa.org

CWA works to strengthen the traditional family according to Judeo-Christian moral standards. It opposes feminism, affirmative action, and the granting of additional civil rights protections to homosexuals. It publishes numerous brochures and policy papers as well as *Family Voice*, a monthly newsmagazine.

**Eagle Forum**
PO Box 618, Alton, IL 62002
(618) 462-5415 • fax: (618) 462-8909
e-mail: eagle@eagleforum.org • website: www.eagleforum.org

The Eagle Forum is dedicated to preserving traditional family values. It believes mothers should stay at home with their children, and it favors policies that reduce government intervention in family issues. The forum opposes feminism, affirmative action, and legislation that promotes special rights for homosexuals. The organization publishes the monthlies *Phyllis Schlafly Report* and *Education Reporter*.

**Heritage Foundation**
214 Massachusetts Ave. NE, Washington, DC 20002-4999
(202) 546-4400 • fax: (202) 546-8328
e-mail: info@heritage.org • website: www.heritage.org

The Heritage Foundation is a public policy research institute that advocates limited government and the free market system. It opposes affirmative action and believes the private sector, not government, should be relied upon to ease social problems and improve the status of women and minorities. The foundation publishes the bimonthly journal *Policy Review* as well as hundreds of monographs, books, and papers on public policy issues.

**Hispanic Policy Development Project (HPDP)**
1001 Connecticut Ave. NW, Suite 901, Washington, DC 20036
(202) 822-8414 • fax: (202) 822-9120

HPDP encourages the analysis of public policies affecting Hispanics in the United States, particularly the education, training, and employment of Hispanic youth. It publishes a number of books and pamphlets, including *Together Is Better: Building Strong Partnerships Between Schools and Hispanic Parents*.

## Lambda Legal Defense and Education Fund
120 Wall St., Suite 1500, New York, NY 10005
(212) 809-8585 • fax: (212) 809-0055
website: www.lambdalegal.org

Lambda is a public-interest law firm committed to achieving full recognition of the civil rights of lesbians, gay men, and people with HIV/AIDS. The firm addresses a variety of topics, including equal marriage rights, employment discrimination, and domestic-partner benefits. It publishes the quarterly *Lambda Update* as well as numerous pamphlets and position papers.

## Male Liberation Foundation (MLF)
701 NE 67th St., Miami, FL 33138
(305) 756-6249 • fax: (305) 756-7962

MLF is a men's organization dedicated to counteracting feminist influence. It aims to inform men that women now hold more power and money than men do, to motivate young men to achieve the career success that young women have, and to encourage women to be housewives. MLF believes men and women have distinct biological and psychological differences, and it opposes all affirmative action legislation. The foundation publishes the monthly newsletter *Male Liberation Foundation* and a book titled *The First Book on Male Liberation and Sex Equality*.

## National Association for the Advancement of Colored People (NAACP)
4805 Mt. Hope Dr., Baltimore, MD 21215-3297
(410) 358-8900 • fax: (410) 486-9257
website: www.naacp.org

The NAACP is the oldest and largest civil rights organization in the United States. Its principal objective is to ensure the political, educational, social, and economic equality of minorities. It publishes the magazine *Crisis* ten times a year as well as a variety of newsletters, books, and pamphlets.

## National Network for Immigrant and Refugee Rights (NNIRR)
310 Eighth St., Suite 303, Oakland, CA 94607
(510) 465-1984 • fax: (510) 465-1885
e-mail: nnirr@nnirr.org • website: www.nnirr.org

The network includes community, church, labor, and legal groups committed to the cause of equal rights for all immigrants. These groups work to end discrimination and unfair treatment of illegal immigrants and refugees. It publishes a monthly newsletter, *Network News*.

## National Organization for Women (NOW)
733 15th St. NW, 2nd Floor, Washington, DC 20005
(202) 628-8NOW (8669) • fax: (202) 785-8576
e-mail: now@now.org • website: www.now.org

NOW is one of the largest and most influential feminist organizations in the United States. It seeks to end prejudice and discrimination against women in all areas of life. NOW lobbies legislatures to make laws more equitable and works to educate and inform the public on women's issues. It publishes the *National NOW Times*, policy statements, and articles.

## National Urban League
120 Wall St., 8th Fl., New York, NY 10005
(212) 558-5300 • fax: (212) 344-5332
website: www.nul.org

A community service agency, the National Urban League aims to eliminate institutional racism in the United States. It also provides services for minorities who experience discrimination in employment, housing, welfare, and other areas. It publishes the report *The Price: A Study of the Costs of Racism in America* and the annual *State of Black America*.

## Parents, Families, and Friends of Lesbians and Gays (PFLAG)
1101 14th St. NW, Suite 1030, Washington, DC 20005
(202) 638-4200 • fax: (202) 638-0243
e-mail: info@pflag.org • website: www.pflag.org

PFLAG is a national organization that provides support and educational services for gays, lesbians, bisexuals, and their families and friends. It works to end prejudice and discrimination against homosexual and bisexual persons. It publishes and distributes books and papers, including "About Our Children," "Coming Out to My Parents," and "Why Is My Child Gay?"

## Poverty and Race Research Action Council (PRRAC)
3000 Connecticut Ave. NW, Suite 200, Washington, DC 20008
(202) 387-9887 • fax: (202) 387-0764
e-mail: info@prrac.org

The Poverty and Race Research Action Council is a nonpartisan, national, not-for-profit organization convened by major civil rights, civil liberties, and antipoverty groups. PRRAC's purpose is to link social science research to advocacy work in order to successfully address problems at the intersection of race and poverty. Its bimonthly publication, *Poverty and Race*, often includes articles on race- and income-based inequities in the United States.

## The Prejudice Institute
Stephens Hall Annex, TSU, Towson, MD 21204-7097
(410) 830-2435 • fax: (410) 830-2455

The Prejudice Institute is a national research center concerned with violence and intimidation motivated by prejudice. It conducts research, supplies information on model programs and legislation, and provides education and training to combat prejudicial violence. The Prejudice Institute publishes research reports, bibliographies, and the quarterly newsletter *Forum*.

## Sojourners
2401 15th St. NW, Washington, DC 20009
(202) 328-8842 • (800) 714-7474 • fax: (202) 328-8757
e-mail: sojourners@sojourners.com
website: www.sojourners.com

Sojourners is an ecumenical Christian organization commited to racial justice and reconciliation between the races. It publishes *America's Original Sin: A Study and Guide on White Racism* as well as the monthly *Sojourners* magazine.

## Third Wave Foundation
116 E. 16th St., 7th Floor, New York, NY 10003
(212) 388-1898 • fax: (212) 982-3321
e-mail: info@thirdwavefoundation.org
website: www.thirdwavefoundation.org

Third Wave is a national organization created by and for young women with the goal of building a lasting foundation for feminist activism around the country. It is led by a diverse board of activist young women and men, and it strives to combat inequalities based on age, gender, race, sexual orientation, economic status, and level of education. The organization publishes the newsletter *See it? Tell it. Change it!*

## United States Commission on Civil Rights
624 Ninth St. NW, Suite 500, Washington, DC 20425
(202) 376-7533 • publications: (202) 376-8128

A fact-finding body, the commission reports directly to Congress and the president on the effectiveness of equal opportunity laws and programs. A catalog of its numerous publications can be obtained from its Publication Management Division.

# Bibliography of Books

Rodolfo Acuna — *Sometimes There Is No Other Side: Chicanos and the Myth of Equality.* Notre Dame, IN: University of Notre Dame Press, 1998.

Maurianne Adams et al., eds. — *Readings for Diversity and Social Justice: An Anthology on Racism, Sexism, Anti-Semitism, Heterosexism, Classism, and Ableism.* New York: Routledge, 2000.

James A. Banks — *An Introduction to Multicultural Education.* Boston: Allyn and Bacon, 1999.

Annie S. Barnes — *Everyday Racism: A Book for All Americans.* Naperville, IL: Sourcebooks, 2000.

Maurice Berger — *White Lies: Race and the Myths of Whiteness.* New York: Farrar, Straus, & Giroux, 1999.

Francine D. Blau and Lawrence M. Kahn — *Gender Differences in Pay.* Cambridge, MA: National Bureau of Economic Research, 2000.

Bob Blauner — *Still the Big News: Racial Oppression in America.* Philadelphia: Temple University Press, 2001.

William G. Bowen and Derek Curtis Bok — *The Shape of the River: Long-Term Consequences of Considering Race in College and University Admissions.* Princeton, NJ: Princeton University Press, 1998.

Chris Bull and John Gallagher — *Perfect Enemies: The Battle Between the Religious Right and the Gay Movement.* Lanham, MD: Madison Books, 2001.

John H. Bunzel — *Affirmative Action in Higher Education: A Dilemma of Conflicting Principles.* Stanford, CA: Hoover Institution, 1998.

Robert D. Cherry — *Who Gets the Good Jobs?: Combating Race and Gender Disparities.* New Brunswick, NJ: Rutgers University Press, 2001.

Samuel Cohn — *Race and Gender Discrimination at Work.* Boulder, CO: Westview Press, 2000.

Dalton Conley — *Honky.* New York: Vintage, 2001.

Ward Connerly — *Creating Equal: My Fight Against Racial Preferences.* San Francisco: Encounter Books, 2000.

Ellis Cose — *Color-Blind: Seeing Beyond Race in a Race-Obsessed World.* New York: HarperPerennial, 1998.

Gerhard Falk — *Stigma: How We Treat Outsiders.* Amherst, NY: Prometheus Books, 2001.

Joe R. Feagin — *Racist America: Roots, Current Realities, and Future Reparations.* New York: Routledge, 2000.

Walter Feinberg

*On Higher Ground: Education and the Case for Affirmative Action.* New York: Teachers College Press, 1998.

Diana Furchtgott-Roth and Christine Stolba

*The Feminist Dilemma: When Success Is Not Enough.* Washington, DC: AEI Press, 2001.

Jim Goad

*The Redneck Manifesto: How Hillbillies, Hicks, and White Trash Became America's Scapegoats.* New York: Simon and Schuster, 1998.

Judi Gold and Susan Vilları, eds.

*Just Sex: Students Rewrite the Rules on Sex, Violence, Activism, and Equality.* Lanham, MD: Rowman and Littlefield, 2000.

Mary B. Harris, ed.

*School Experiences of Gay and Lesbian Youth: The Invisible Minority.* New York: Harrington Park Press, 1997.

Gregory M. Herek

*Stigma and Sexual Orientation: Understanding Prejudice Against Lesbians, Gay Men, and Bisexuals.* Thousand Oaks, CA: Sage, 1998.

Thomas C. Holt

*The Problem of Race in the Twenty-First Century.* Cambridge, MA: Harvard University Press, 2000.

David Horowitz

*Hating Whitey and Other Progressive Causes.* Dallas: Spence, 1999.

Tahar Ben Jelloun et al.

*Racism Explained to My Daughter.* New York: New Press, 1999.

June Jordan

*Affirmative Acts: Political Essays.* New York: Anchor Books, 1998.

Mary C. King, ed.

*Squaring Up: Policy Strategies to Raise Women's Income in the United States.* Ann Arbor: University of Michigan Press, 2001.

Elisabeth Lasch-Quinn

*Race Experts: How Racial Etiquette, Sensitivity Training, and New Age Therapy Hijacked the Civil Rights Revolution.* New York: W.W. Norton, 2001.

Anne C. Levy and Michele A. Paludi

*Workplace Sexual Harassment.* Upper Saddle River, NJ: Prentice-Hall, 2002.

Don C. Locke

*Increasing Multicultural Understanding: A Comprehensive Model.* Thousand Oaks, CA: Sage, 1998.

Donald MacEdo and Lilia I. Bartolome

*Dancing with Bigotry: Beyond the Politics of Tolerance.* New York: St. Martin's Press, 2001.

Eileen O'Brien

*Whites Confront Racism: Antiracists and Their Paths to Action.* Lanham, MD: Rowman and Littlefield, 2001.

Gary Orfield and Edward Miller

*Chilling Admissions: The Affirmative Action Crisis and the Search for Alternatives.* Cambridge, MA: Harvard Education Publishing Group, 1998.

Patti Paniccia

*Work Smarts for Women: The Essential Sex Discrimination Survival Guide.* New York: Ballantine Books, 2000.

Barbara F. Reskin

*The Realities of Affirmative Action in Employment.* Washington, DC: American Sociological Association, 1998.

Jo Ann Ooiman Robinson

*Affirmative Action: A Documentary History.* Westport, CT: Greenwood, 2001.

Paula S. Rothenberg, ed.

*Race, Class, and Gender in the United States: An Integrated Study.* New York: St. Martin's Press, 1998.

Alvin J. Schmidt

*The Menace of Multiculturalism: Trojan Horse in America.* Westport, CT: Praeger, 1997.

Diane Silver

*The New Civil War: The Lesbian and Gay Struggle for Civil Rights.* Danbury, CT: Franklin Watts, 1997.

Shelby Steele

*A Dream Deferred: The Second Betrayal of Black Freedom in America.* New York: HarperCollins, 1998.

Stephen Steinberg

*Turning Back: The Retreat from Racial Justice in American Thought and Policy.* Boston: Beacon Press, 2001.

Leonard Steinhorn and Barbara Diggs-Brown

*By the Color of Our Skin: The Illusion of Integration and the Reality of Race.* New York: Penguin, 1999.

Stephan Thernstrom and Abigail Thernstrom

*America in Black and White: One Nation, Indivisible.* New York: Simon and Schuster, 1997.

Becky W. Thompson

*A Promise and a Way of Life: White Antiracist Activism.* Minneapolis: University of Minnesota Press, 2001.

James Waller

*Prejudice Across America.* Jackson: University of Mississippi, 2000.

Lena Williams and Charlayne Hunter-Gault

*It's the Little Things: The Everyday Interactions That Get Under the Skin of Blacks and Whites.* San Diego: Harcourt Trade, 2000.

Patricia J. Williams

*Seeing a Color-Blind Future: The Paradox of Race.* New York: Noonday Press, 1998.

# Index

Aetna insurance, 194
affirmative action
  academic performance and, 115, 134
  *Bakke* case on, 129–31
  black stereotypes and, 78
  challenges to, 105–106, 131–32
  criticism of, 71
  diversity and, 117, 121–24, 128–29,
    132–34, 135–36
  does not correct discrimination, 115,
    117
  eliminating, 77, 128
    challenge of, 124–25
    does not end racial division,
      125–26
    as harming businesses, 109–10
    school resegregation and, 110–11
  equal opportunity and, 111
  immigrants helped by, 119–20
  as most effective remedy to
    discrimination, 108–109
  necessity of, 110
  point system for college admissions,
    70–72, 134–35
  preferential treatment through, 69–70
  "qualified" applicants and, 114
  quotas, 105, 115
  race as overwhelming factor in,
    113–14
  race/sex discrimination as being
    wrong under, 114–15
  roots of, 105
  seen in context of racial
    disadvantages, 74–76
  standardized tests and, 116
  supported by head of Office of Civil
    Rights, 200–201
  as a threat to equality, 116
African Americans
  crime by, 14, 28, 177–78
  discrimination of, compared with
    other minorities, 24
  earnings of female, 47
  as getting beyond race, 33–34
  in interracial marriage, 34–36
  laying down the burden of race,
    32–33
  racial hostility by, 93–95
  on racial pride, 94
  on racial profiling, 173–74
  racial wounds of, 142–43
  on reparations for slavery, 193
  slavery did not cause economic and
    cultural ills of, 191
  stereotypes of, 78, 174–75

  *see also* minorities; reparations for
    slavery
Albright, Madeleine, 108
Alpert, Rebecca T., 85
American Civil Liberties Union
  (ACLU), 13, 27, 54
American Dream, the, 198
Amirall-Padamse, Irma, 153, 156
Anderson, Mark, 52–53
Anderson, William, 160
Angelou, Maya, 147–48
antigay job discrimination
  broadening imagination of America
    and, 201–202
  equal opportunity for all and, 199
  fighting against, vs. fighting for
    other equal rights, 205–206
  incidences of, 52–53, 55–56
  is not a pressing issue for gays and
    lesbians, 204–205
  legislation opposing, 52, 54–55, 61–62
  rights for all Americans and, 198–99
  "special rights" protection and, 204
Arredondo, Earl, 23
Ashcroft, John, 171, 174
Asian Americans
  discrimination of, 20, 24, 120–21
  helped by affirmative action, 119–20
  racial profiling of, 20
  on racial stereotypes, 123
  reparations for, 183
  *see also* minorities
Astin, Alexander, 123
Attwood, Polly, 54–55
AutoNation USA, 55–56
Ayvazian, Andrea, 141

*Baker v. State of Vermont*, 62
Bakhtin, Mikhail, 102
Bakke, Allan, 105, 129, 132
*Bakke* case, 71–72, 105, 129, 129–31,
  132
Balmer, Katherine, 151
Banks, James A., 66
Barko, Naomi, 49
Barlaz, Hinda Adele, 154–55
Barr, Ali, 24
Barton, Janice, 83
black middle-class rage, 20
blacks. *See* African Americans
*Blue Eyed* (film), 153
Bobo, Lawrence, 17, 20, 24
Bok, Derek, 134
Bowen, William G., 134
Bradley, Bill, 171–72

219